The Jewish Creedal Prayer

Shema Yisroel, adonai *elohenu,* adonai *echod.*
"Hear (and obey), O Israel, the Lord our God, the Lord is One."
Deuteronomy 6:4, Mark 12:29

A Mormon's Guide to Judaism

Introduction to Jewish religion and culture for Latter-day Saints

Compiled and edited by
Marlena Tanya Muchnick
with Daniel C. Baker

D1571555

For further information, contact the author at:

www.jewishconvert-lds.com or
marlenamuchnick@yahoo.com

Cover design:
Kim Packard Cooney dba Byzintek
15843 SE 47th Street
Bellevue, Washington 98006-3264 USA
kim.cooney@comcast.net
www.byzintek.com
tel. 425.643.2330

Distributed by:
Granite Publishing and Distribution, L.L.C.
1-800-574-5779

Acknowledgement

I am grateful to the providers of the essential material for this book. It has been gleaned from numerous sources both ancient and current. Research information is listed in the last section.

Thanks also to the editors and contributors who gave of their time and expertise, including Rav Dovid Robins and Alan Steele.

Without the help of my husband, Daniel, this Guide could not have been completed. His technical expertise, insight and suggestions were essential to the scope of this work and are deeply appreciated.

The Testimony of a Jew

"Is it crazy to say that the conversion of a Jewish soul is the culmination of the wanderings of ancient Jews who followed Abraham and Moses out of hellish Egypt? My own family's ancestors lived as hunted animals in the wartime ghettos of Europe. They came looking for freedom but ended being herded like cattle across Germany in the killing boxcars. They endured bravely the stuffy, overloaded boats that bore them on the last leg of their Diaspora and brought them to a waiting America that they might worship in freedom.

They came here also for me, that I, too, might worship in freedom. I carried with me their darkness, their unrelieved yearning for the light the full Gospel brings. My future would now be filled with the bright light of Christ and the further assurance that I was finally in his Church. In the sacred moments of baptism by one having true authority, then the laying on of hands for the reception of the gift of the Holy Ghost, it was made known to me that I had learned the ways of God at Jesus' feet! As a new Christian I would be required to follow him in all things as one of the many thousands of missionaries of the Restoration, to progress in my life's journey until that day when I should hopefully meet him again at that Bar of eternal judgment.

There are souls who love the Lord with only a part of their being, seemingly in little need of spiritual nourishment. But to a Jew who loves God more than life and longs for the saving grace of a personal Savior and the guiding ministrations of the great Comforter, even the Holy Spirit, The Church of Jesus Christ of Latter-day Saints is the coming home, the bringing forward out of silent darkness into brilliant light truths that are saving and eternal. To me, this is the fulfillment of any life. The full Gospel contains all that anyone needs to know of Christ and his truth at the current time because Christ is its living head. It is a table spread before the faithful searcher, filled with survival food for the soul. It is, simply, the perfect feast."

From *Life Changing Testimonies of the Lord Jesus Christ* by Marlena Tanya Muchnick

Contents

Preface

Many members and missionaries of the Church of Jesus Christ of Latter-day Saints have approached me in the Temple, at church meetings, or at firesides asking for information about Judaism. They want to understand the many facets of Jewish thought, worship, culture and history of these people to better communicate with Jewish co-workers, neighbors and friends with greater knowledge and confidence.

Is it important? The scriptures and latter-day prophets say that it is.

Ezra Taft Benson, one of the presidents of the Church of Jesus Christ of Latter-day Saints (1985-1994) has said "**We need to know more about the Jews, and the Jews ought to know more about the Mormons.**" *(See To Judah from Joseph, page 98)*

In response to continuing demand, this Guide has evolved from a two-page handout to a significant index of information. It is divided into three parts to help the reader find general or specific knowledge:

Part One - an overall, basic view of Jewish beliefs and special holidays. Particular focus is directed toward development of cultural understanding between Jew and Gentile.

Part Two - more detail on these themes, with an LDS perspective.

Part Three - reference material. Tables, indices and glossaries for those with special interest in the history of Israel, Hebrew and Hebraisms, holidays, rituals, scholars, prophecies, Jewish jokes and recipes.

This guide is for anyone who wants to know more about Judaism, including the Jewish people! Brief synopses of significant aspects of Judaism are included to help you understand Jewish ways, ideas and some significant linguistic principles of the Hebrew language. You will be better prepared to fellowship the Jewish mind and spirit, to converse with Jews with appropriate, insightful and timely information. You will be able to overcome objections raised to the Gospel by your Jewish associates, investigators and neighbors. It will also help them to more fully appreciate their own spiritual heritage and culture. *Feel free to share this book with them.*

The Prophet Joseph Studied Hebrew and Jewish Culture

In the "History of The Church", daily entries from November 21, 1835 to March 25, 1836 show that the Prophet led several apostles in the reading and studying of Hebrew. They believed it was very important they know these ancient writings firsthand. The Mormon Hebrew School was in the translating room in the upper part of the Kirtland Temple. A Hebrew teacher, a rabbi (his name was *Yeshua*) was eventually hired. On January 4th they divided the school into classes. On January 19th Joseph said "It seems as if the Lord opens our minds in a marvelous manner, to understand His word in the original language." He eventually translated some scriptures into Hebrew.

The Prophet and his apostles desired to more "fully understand the new revelations" promised and issuing forth from the Lord as his house, his temple, approached its dedication". *The Holy Land Idea in American Spiritual History*, in *With Eyes Toward Zion: (Moshe Davis, Scholars Colloquium on America-Holy Land Studies.)*

Joseph Smith's Dedicatory Prayer of March 27 is particularly significant:

Now these words, O Lord, we have spoken before thee, concerning the revelations and commandments which thou has given unto us, who are identified with the Gentiles. But thou knowest that thou hast a great love for the children of Jacob, who have been scattered upon the mountains for a long time, in a cloudy and dark day. We therefore ask thee to have mercy upon the children of Jacob, that Jerusalem, from this hour, may begin to be redeemed; And the yoke of bondage may begin to be broken off from the house of David; And the children of Judah may begin to return to the lands which thou didst give to Abraham their father (D&C 109:60-63).

In every instance the Lord's words pointed toward a fulfillment that Jewish law would never approach, because his way is ennobling, not merely lawful. The doctrine of Jesus Christ is set forth in power and simplicity in 3 NE 11:31-34; Mark 16:15,16 and John 12:48.

Oh ye Gentiles, have ye remembered the Jews, mine ancient covenant people: Nay; but ye have cursed them, and have hated them, and have not sought to recover them. But behold, I will return all these things upon your own heads; for I the Lord have not forgotten my people." (2 Nephi 29:4-5, Book of Mormon)

New and exciting avenues of understanding can come from the loving sharing of the cultural, linguistic, racial and religious beliefs of Jews and "Gentiles" *(See Glossary)*. Let these advance the bringing together the families, rather than the "stick" of Judah with the "stick" of Ephraim *(Ezek 37:16-22)*.

May the Lord bless you in your honest desires to understand and to love your Jewish brethren!

Judah's Blessing:

Judah is a lion's whelp: from the prey, my son, thou art gone up: he stooped down; he couched as a lion, and as an old lion; who shall rouse him up? The scepter shall not depart from Judah, nor a lawgiver from between his feet, until Shiloh come; and unto him shall the gathering of the people be.

Binding his foal unto the vine, and his ass's colt unto the choice vine; he washed his garments in wine, and his clothes in the blood of grapes:

His eyes shall be red with wine, and his teeth white with milk. (Genesis 49:9-12).

Joseph's Blessing:

Joseph is a fruitful bough, even a fruitful bough by a well; whose branches run over the wall: The archers have sorely grieved him, and shot at him, and hated him: But his bow abode in strength, and the arms of his hands were made strong by the hands of the mighty God of Jacob; (from thence is the shepherd, the stone of Israel:)

Even by the God of thy father, who shall help thee; and by the Almighty, who shall bless thee with blessings of heaven above, blessings of the deep that lieth under, blessings of the breast, and of the womb;

The blessings of thy father have prevailed above the blessings of my progenitors unto the utmost bound of the everlasting hills: they shall be on the head of Joseph, and on the crown of the head of him that was separate from his brethren. (Genesis 49:22-26)

Introduction

Surely the Lord God will do nothing, but he revealeth his secret unto his servants the prophets. Amos 3:7

Jewish culture and religious practices are derived from centuries of wanderings in lands other than Israel. However, they are rich in history, liturgy, superstition, belief in old world customs, biblically determined laws affecting behavior, agriculture, worship, commerce, etc. Judaism is much more than a culture or religion; it is a sub-civilization, an interlinked network of people, ideas, history, territory, activities, languages, property, liturgy, songs, hundreds of daily and holiday ritualistic practices, allegiance to ancient beliefs and practices and a special fellowship that embraces every Jew as a family member.

Primarily for these reasons and with the noticeable exception of the growing number of Messianic congregations, the Jewish people are not interested in investigating other religions, especially Christianity. They are usually quite happy knowing and practicing what they believe. Though they are the people from whom Jesus or *Yeshua* of Nazareth descended, Jews do not regard him as divine, holy or as their Savior and Messiah (**Moshiach**).

Jews rarely convert to Christianity. When they do, their families often disown them or treat them with great disdain. To many Jews, the mere idea of Jesus Christ as anything more than a teacher of truth, is reprehensible. It is a threat to Jewish identity to even think of merging a Jewish lifestyle with anything Christian. Many Jews disdain the very words "Jesus Christ" and become quite upset when those of a Christian faith approach them with ideas of teaching or conversion. Jews are essentially resistant to change in this way because they also fear angering God who, they have been taught, forbids the inclusion or worship of any other gods and idols. This can make approaching a Jewish person with the purpose of introducing the Gospel of Christ a very difficult endeavor.

Those who meet and wish to fellowship a Jew are encouraged to learn about Judaism first. One needs to know somewhat of a Jewish turn of mind; their cultural and religious experiences. Have they any worldly understanding that would signal an opportunity to take an independent and thoughtful interest in this most touchy of subjects? That is for the Christian friend to assess.

The Jewish people revere the pursuit and accumulation of knowledge. They appreciate a non-Jew who is conversant with Jewish culture, practices, language, etc. To help the learner, Hebrew names are listed for some significant biblical characters. Practice pronouncing the names in Hebrew. Your Jewish investigator will respect you for your efforts and hopefully assist you in learning more!

Jewish people want to be approached with approval and understanding, perhaps more than people of Protestant religions. As monotheistic worshippers who believe their spiritual and mortal lives are off limits to anyone seeking to bring Christianity or other persuasions into play, the non-Jew must truly pique an interest and provoke honest interest in new knowledge and spiritual experience. One of the thoughts that allowed the author to drop some defensive barriers when stake missionaries wanted to visit was the idea that she would have to "give up nothing, but only acquire more knowledge". Eventually, of course, old ways are given up to make joyous affirmation from the messages of the Holy Ghost who can newly make the Jewish investigator in the image of a true believer in the Lord Jesus Christ. Your investigator will always be a Jew, but more importantly, *he or she will also know his Mashiach and the restored Kingdom, i.e. Church.*

Get to know your Jewish neighbor as a child of God, a friend, and a unique individual. Ask about his beliefs and seek to share those religious, cultural and spiritual experiences. Involve yourself in his life and activities as permissible to set your friend at ease. Learn some Yiddish or Hebrew and what you can about Jewish holidays, prayers, etc. The Jewish people are essentially involved with the experiences of day-to-day living. They relate to life in physical, earthy terms. That is the best way to approach them. Be sure to bring some humor with you. Humor, especially simple Jewish jokes will go far to lower barriers of suspicion and mistrust.

After reading this book you will have sufficient knowledge to start and continue conversations, research and discover on your own, and to make strides in presenting your side of things to the edification of your Jewish brethren. Time is not of consequence, I might add.

Your work may not pay off for years or not at all. But if you are finally successful in bringing understanding of the life and mission of Jesus/*Yeshua* to a Jewish soul, your reward will be multifold, for Jews who love their Savior are of the most devoted, productive, appreciative and joyous kind.

Do not give up. Your mission is urgently necessary and ultimately will bring saving ordinances to a people living happily blind to their own potential. *(See Romans 11:8-10,25.)*

Part 1: Basic Understanding

This section introduces a basic understanding about the more common practices and beliefs of your Jewish friends. Some of the topics in this section are:

Linguistic Considerations

The Jewish Spirit

What Is a Jew?

What Is Judaism?

What Do Jews Believe?

How To Build a Bridge

Tips for Opening Dialogues

Differences between Judaism and LDS

Similarities between Judaism and LDS

Worship and Religious Practices

Jewish Congregations: Summary

Major Expressions of Judaism

Major Jewish Holidays

For detailed study, please proceed to Part 2 after you read this section.

Linguistic Considerations

Hebrew is an ancient Semitic language related to Aramaic and nearest to the ancient Adamic language. It was codified around 600 B.C., when Lehi left Jerusalem. Many characteristics come from ancient Egyptian hieroglyphics and pictograms. Both languages were spoken in *Torah* times. It has always been a living language. Hebrew is read from right to left. Hebrew names in the *Torah* and the Book of Mormon have meanings that may include messages. These meanings are interesting. For instance, "Adam" means "man", "Israel" means "prevailed with God", and "Lehi" means "for/to life", whereas "*l'chayim*" means to/for eternal life in Hebrew.

The names Abram and Abraham are spelled as "Avram" and "Avraham" in this guide to show the correct Hebrew pronunciation, except where a quote contains the common spelling. When a choice between the B or V is available, this author uses "V", the Hebrew equivalent, to help readers immerse themselves in Jewish culture and language.

Each Hebrew character has multiple meanings. The various shapes of some Hebrew letters refer to ideas and physical things. Hebrew is a language derived from letters which originally represented physical objects. An understanding of how this works in word groups brings the reader a fuller understanding of the language.

You will notice variations in spelling in certain Hebrew words in this book. Hebrew has no vowels among the 22 letters of its alphabet, but when spoken, vowelization takes place. Therefore, pronunciations and spellings vary among non-Hebrew speaking peoples due to linguistic differences. As an example, the Hebrew *ma-SHEE-ach* or Messiah can be pronounced *mashiach*, *meshiach* or *moshiach*.

Because Hebrew has no letter for "J", the letter and sound of "Y" is correct usage; hence, *Yeshua* and *Yehovah*. The English consonantal pair of "th" is absent in Hebrew, hence the Hebrew words "*urim* and *thummim*" are pronounced as "oo'rim (and) to'mim", meaning light and truth.

For more information on Hebrew, see page 73.

Yiddish is a language based upon German with elements of Polish, Hungarian, Rumanian, Hebrew and Russian. It was the most efficient language for Jews from the 1600's through the First and Second World Wars as a means of communication between the non-Hebrew speaking people of Europe. It is dying out as a modern language, and modern Hebrew is again flourishing. Below are a few emergency Yiddish and Hebrew words.

A hard round roll	*Bagel*	Family	*Mishpocha*
Peace unto you	*Sha**lom** alei**chem***	Father	*Tateh*
Happy holiday	*Gut **Shabbos***	Mother	***Ma**meh*
Congratulations, good luck	***Ma**zel tov*	Grandfather	*Zayde*
To/for eternal, continuous life	*L'cha**yim***	Grandmother	*Bubbe*
Sabbath (Fri nite-Sat nite)	*Shab**bat***	Talk informally	*Kib**butz***
Passover dinner	***Pe**sach seder*	A name of God	*HaShem*

The Jewish Spirit

The gathering of nomadic Semite groups to the lands near the Mediterranean and the Red Sea resulted in the rise of the Hebrew people. From the fall of Judah to the present time these once nomadic families have assimilated into a modern Jewry. While there are many racial variations of Jewry: African, Asian, Caucasian, Japanese, European, Nordic, Spanish, the same lively and dedicated spirit defines them all.

Generally speaking, to be Jewish is to be unique. It has been likened to a collection of twelve families in which only those who embrace a special kind of worship, lifestyle, culture and racial outlook are welcome, though the races, languages and cultures involved may be vastly different. Contributions of Jews to the world are uncountable, but the several most valuable are: *Torah* scriptures, the *Talmud* and *Kaballah* writings, the holy priesthoods, the prophets of God, and the Savior himself: *Yeshua*, which means "Salvation" and refers to Jesus. A seminal principle of the Avrahamic Covenant is that through the Jewish people all the nations of the earth will be blessed. What is there about this people that our Heavenly Father has worked through them to accomplish his will?

Perhaps the answer lies in the nature of the Jewish spirit as caregiver, as householder to the world—*Bet Yisroel*—the House of Israel. Within the spiritual house of Judaism is the love for its members and love for the common traditions that molded them, as well as experiences they share. Jews have an underlying sense of kinship that affects all they say and do. They are a people of charity and duty, of tradition and stubborn changelessness, hope and courage, of fight and forgiveness, of learning and teaching, finance and the power of monetary expansion. They hit the floor of life running. Often their success is due to kinship, knowledge, endurance and hope.

Their hope stems from devotion to their Creator whom they call by numerous names: *(Anciently: En Sof, El, El Shaddai), Adonai, Elohim, HaShem*, the Eternal One. *(See page 31).* They are unaware that Jehovah in the Hebrew *Torah* (Christians call it the "Old Testament") is the same person as Jesus Christ in the New Testament. The Jewish people as a whole are passionate about their love and devotion to our Heavenly Father, for they know they are His Chosen. They believe His eternal covenant with them, this special kinship, sets them truly apart from all others. We can say that this sacred agreement, which the Jews express through *Torah*, is the existential root and core of Jewish being, destiny and function. *(See Torah, page 8.)*

It is through the Jewish spirit and people that latter-day restoration has occurred and flourishes today. Sadly, because Jesus was rejected of his people, they have suffered tragically. But the Lord has promised to redeem them, and the family of Ephraim has been the beneficiary of marvelous and eternal blessings in their stead. *(See LDS Scriptural Citations, page 97).* When they are finally redeemed and partake again of the promises made to them through the Avrahamic Covenant in the temples of God, their ages old **creedal prayer** will take on deeper significance and fulfillment:

> *Hear (and obey), O Israel, the Lord our God, the Lord is One.*
> *(Deut 6:4, Mark 12:29).*

What Is a Jew?

What does it mean to be a Jew? Are they members of a religion, a race, a culture, a geographic group? Most people, both Jewish and Gentile, would instinctively say that Judaism is a religion. They are partly correct. The Jewish people have no clear and concise canon of belief, but they are generally united in their belief in one God.

One reason the Jewish people believe they are unique can be traced to their ancient racial links to Avraham, Isaac, Jacob and Moses, who were Hebrews. A Jew is traditionally born of a Jewish woman, who is born also of a Jewish woman, etc.

Even a child born of a non-Jewish woman but who has a Jewish father (who is usually the son of a Jewish mother) claims the lineage and posterity of Judaism. There are many hundreds of societies of which Jews are a part, and they resemble the culture they were born into. But always their claim to that special heritage sets them apart in their heart, soul and mind.

4

Converts to Judaism may be considered Jews in every sense but one; that of descendency from a biological parent who claims a bloodline from the Israelites.

Another important reason Judaism is unique is the religious affiliations it holds: Jews are monotheistic. They believe in one God because God commanded them to have no other gods before Him *(Gen 20:3)*. They have agreed to be His chosen people. Their worship is always directed to their Heavenly Father who is to them also the Lord of all things, and whose spirit *(Sheckinah)* can sometimes be felt or even seen. In their secular, devoted and often passionate appreciation for God, Jews are encouraged by their families to maintain their separateness from non-Jews in marriage and child bearing, though liberal congregations do not observe this ancient commandment with much regularity.

Origin of the Word "Jew". The word applied to the descendents of Judah, fourth son of Jacob with Leah. The territory of Judah fell to Babylon conquerors in 586 B.C. The word "Jew" is generally used to refer to all people of Israelite descent. All Jews are Israelites, but not all Israelites are Jews, since there were eleven other families beside Judah. *(Gen 43:32, Ex 3:18, 2 Cor 11:22)*. Also, not all Hebrews were Israelites *(Gen 10:25, 16:15)*. Many Jewish people are not familiar with these differences.

Gentile. The term "Gentile" in its original Hebrew context means "*foreigner, stranger, other.*" It does not necessarily mean "non-Jew." It would be wise to more specifically define the word.

1. Descendents of Noah's son Japheth *(Gen 10:1-5)*, Shem or Ham would not be Gentiles because they could trace their lineage to Abraham.

2. Non-descendents of Abraham and Isaac.

3. After the Kingdom of Israel was destroyed, those not of the tribe of Judah were called Gentiles.

4. Non-members of the Church of Jesus Christ of Latter-day Saints, excepting the Jewish people (see 2 above), are Gentiles. Through membership they are adopted by Heavenly Father into the lineage (and blood) of Abraham and eligible to receive the blessings of the Abrahamic Covenant.

Non-Jews are always to some extent the "*goyim*" (meaning both *nation* and *Gentiles*), the outsiders to a Jewish environment. They are incorrectly considered by many Jews to be inferior simply because of their non-inclusion as people born of a Jewish mother or father. Though many of today's Jews know little or nothing of their heritage or prophets, or have read in *Torah* or *Talmud*, their feeling of exclusivity is an invisible barrier to change.

What Is Judaism?

A Nation, a People, a Culture

It is safe to say that Jews feel a sense of connectedness to each other that many find hard to explain, define, or even understand. The best explanation is the traditional one given in *Torah*: that the Jews are a chosen nation. They use the word "nation" not in the modern sense meaning a territorial and political entity, but in the ancient sense meaning a group of people with a common history and a common destiny.

The set of ideas regarding the world and the way in which Jews should live is contained in the practice of Judaism. This guide will discuss the general system of beliefs of the Jewish people throughout the world.

Israel

Within the last dozen years modern day Israel has experienced a growth of a million immigrants, mostly from Russian speaking countries. The latter-day restoration of the Gospel to "Joseph" and the return of the keys of the gathering of Israel that includes both "Joseph and Judah," represent the first fruit in the parable of the fig tree. A remarkable gathering has started. This gathering is reflected in the growth of the Latter-day Saint population as well as the State of Israel, which in the parable of the fig tree is a symbol for the putting forth of leaves *(Book of Mormon, Jacob 5,)*. This gathering is in preparation of the coming of the Redeemer, which in the fig tree parable is the second fruit.

The Jewish Race

Jews have always claimed common ancestry from biological parents known to be of Jewish origin, so they are racially connected through bloodline. Because they claim descent from ancient family groups of Israel, to be Jewish means to be of Semitic origin. This feeling contributes to their secularism. *(See Families of Israel, page 78)*

Wandering Hebrews have mingled, settled and intermarried with the world's populations through time. There are members of racial groups throughout the world who still call themselves Jews. They assert their origin through one of the twelve tribes or families of Israel, descendents of Avraham, Isaac and Jacob. (Note that "Israel" means "ruling with God.)

It is sadly true that many Jews in the United States don't belong to any synagogue, although they may hold beliefs in some ritualistic practices and celebrate some Jewish holidays. It is also true that many Jews have converted to Christianity, Islam, Buddhism, etc. Some Jews claim agnosticism or atheism. **They are still Jews by virtue of their ancestry even though they have embraced other theologies and cultures.**

What Do Jews Believe?

Mosaic Law – Halakhah

Mosaic law is a system of Jewish behavior codified as religious law. The earliest version of the Mosaic Code was part of an ancient tradition of laws discovered in Istanbul and dates from 2050 B.C. *(History of the Jews, page 32)* Other law codes eventually followed. They contained rules and regulations regarding human conduct and legislative treatises on civil, criminal, and moral law. *Halakhah* is Hebrew for Mosaic Law, and means "path" or "way".

The core of Mosaic law is the Decalogue (the Ten Commandments). *See Exodus 20:2-14, Deuteronomy 5:6-18.* This was the basis of the covenant with God first made by Abraham, renewed by Jacob, then by Moses and the Israelites during the Exodus. The Mosaic legal material was organized by Jewish scholars into 613 commandments, consisting of 248 mandatory commandments and 365 prohibitions.

Moses collected and codified these laws. In Mosaic legal theory, all breaches of the law offend God. Offenses are sins, and therefore require restitution and expiation. Whereas Near East codes of law are property oriented, Mosaic law is God-oriented.

For example, the famous dictum "an eye for an eye," etc. means only that strict compensation for the injury is due. *See also: Pharisees Tampered with Mosaic Law, page 42.*

Paul wrote that Mosaic Law as taught by Hebrew prophets was only "a schoolmaster to bring us to Christ" *(Gal 3:24). This body of laws was never referred to as an everlasting Covenant*, so it had to be that the church Jesus Christ established would make up the lack. Why? Because Christ's law is superior. Several examples will help us to understand the difference.

"Whereas the law forbade murder, and provided a just penalty for the crime, Christ taught that one's giving way to anger, which might ... lead to violence or even murder, was of itself a sin.

"The law forbade the awful sin of adultery; Christ said that the sin began in the lustful glance, the sensual thought; and He added that it was better to become blind than to look with the evil eye..." Jesus the Christ, James E. Talmage, pp 218-21.

The Lord also spoke to the transitory nature of worldly wealth. Referring to the rich Pharisees whose almsgivings were small but publically displayed, Jesus taught instead the enduring riches of eternity. Wealth can be destroyed by the elements, but "infinitely more precious are the treasures of a life well spent, the wealth of good deeds, the account of which is kept in heaven where the riches of righteous achievement are safe... *"For where your treasure is, there will your heart be also."* Luke *12:34. (Quoted in Jesus the Christ, James E. Talmage, pp. 218-21.)*

Torah

Torah might be considered the core of Jewish belief. *Torah*—the Law—is equated or considered life itself, to a devout Jew. It is read virtually continuously. *Torah* scrolls are considered sacred and handled with the ultimate reverence and protection.

Torah (Pentateuch) means "a teaching". It contains the first five books of Moses, Genesis, Exodus, Leviticus, Numbers and Deuteronomy (second law). It has two sections, written and oral. It is not the same nor has it the same contents as a standard Bible, regardless of translation. *Oral Torah*, a specific work, was formulated by rabbis in the first few centuries A.D. These traditions had to be transmitted orally. Each book is called a *chumash.*

Because of their acceptance of *Torah*, Jews believe they have a special status in the eyes of God, but can lose it if *Torah* is abandoned. The blessings received by accepting *Torah* mean they feel a greater obligation to God than non-Jews because they are responsible for fulfilling the 613 *mitzvot* (commandments) in *Torah*. Some Jews believe God will punish them for doing things that would not be a sin for non-Jews.

Jewish scriptural canon also contains the books of the prophets and other writings, often printed in a second book; i.e., Psalms, Proverbs, Job, Song of Songs, Ruth, Lamentations, Ecclesiastes, Esther, Daniel, Ezra and Nehemiah and Chronicles (24 books). The set is referred to as the **Tanakh,** an acronym for *Torah* (**law**), *Nevi'im* (**prophets**) and *Ketuvi'im* (**writings**). *(More: page 40)*

There is a tradition in Judaism that Moses composed part of the book of Deuteronomy. *(See Deut 31:9)* The *Mishnah Torah* is this portion. It is composed in rabbinic Hebrew and divided into fourteen general sections, each of which is further subdivided into books (like tractates), and then into numbered chapters and laws.

Talmud

A written work comprised of Jewish oral law, (*Mishnah*) was codified in A.D.220. The *Gemara* text is rabbinic scholarly commentary on the *Mishnah,* compiled between the 2nd and 5th centuries A.D. *Mishnah* is made up of six sections, each called a **seder** (order) and containing tracts. The sections are: laws of agriculture, prayer, blessings, holidays, laws of marriage and divorce, civil law, sacrifices, and laws of purity and ritual impurity. There is a Jerusalem and a Babylonian *Talmud.*

Talmudic scripture is sacred to Jewry. Written by sages, scholars and rabbis, it claims to cover all of humanity's situations. It is a vast work of intellect and opinion, the opinions of learned men. It has influenced the culture and literature, the philosophy and daily life of all pious Jews throughout the centuries. Many themes are similar to LDS scripture and commentary upon the nature of God and mankind, how God and Satan perform in the universe, doctrines on sin and salvation, goodness and duty, the Commandments, moral and domestic life, meaning and purpose of death, etc. These writings are often in agreement with those of mainline religious groups because virtue and holiness are continually stressed. But they are interwoven with mystery, fantasy, folklore, and stories. The *Talmud* is fascinating reading, but contradictory opinions do abound. *(More: page 42)*

Life

In Judaism, life is valued above all other mortal concerns except devotion to God. The *Talmud* notes that all people are descended from a single person, Avraham. Thus, taking a single life is like destroying an entire world, and saving a single life is like saving an entire world.

Judaism not only permits but often *requires* a person to violate the commandments if necessary to save a life. Doctors are permitted to answer emergency calls on *Shabbat* (Sabbath), even though this may violate many *Shabbat* prohibitions. *(More: page 45)*

Death

Jews look upon death as a natural process. In Judaism, death is not a tragedy, even when it occurs early in life or through unfortunate circumstances. Death, like life, has meaning and is part of God's plan. Jews believe in an afterlife where good deeds are rewarded but they have no clear idea of what an "afterlife" promises or how to prepare for it on earth.

See Care for Dead and Mourning on page 134 for detail on those subjects.

Resurrection and Reincarnation

Belief in the eventual resurrection of the dead *(Daniel 12:2)*, *Tikkun-olam*, is a fundamental belief of traditional Judaism although it is not found in the Pentateuch. It was a belief that distinguished the Pharisees (intellectual ancestors of rabbi*nical* Judaism) from the Sadducees. The second blessing of the *Shemoneh Esrei* prayer (*sh'MOH-neh ES-ray*) (meaning "eighteen"), which is recited three times daily, contains several references to resurrection. The Reform movement, which apparently rejects this belief, has rewritten the second blessing. *(More: page 45)*

Interfaith Marriages

Traditional Judaism does not permit interfaith marriages. *Torah* states that the children of such marriages would be lost to Judaism *(Deut. 7:3-4)*, though Avraham was a convert, as were all of the matriarchs of Judaism. The Moabite Ruth was an ancestor of King David. Children of intermarriage are rarely raised Jewish; they are normally raised Christian or non-religious. Jews view intermarriage as a serious breach of loyalty to a royal heritage. One Orthodox Jew went so far as to state an extreme view that intermarriage is accomplishing what Hitler could not: the destruction of the Jewish people.

Satan

God's only Adversary, surrounded by his evil minions. From Persian thought. Zoroaster believed in conflicts between good, evil, light and darkness. Jews are very superstitious regarding the "Other One". They have phrases to ward off evil that are repeated at certain times to defeat or keep out the Evil One. For example: "God forbid it" is uttered as "*kineahora*" (kin a hora). When the dead are mentioned, the deceased's name is followed by "May he rest in peace". According to Jewish belief, Satan will eventually be rebuked by God and destroyed, making unnecessary any verbal precautions.

What About Jesus? Jehovah? Messiah?

Jews do not believe that Jesus was the *Moshiach*. Assuming that the Christian scriptures are accurate in describing him, they believe he did not fulfill the mission of the *Moshiach* or fulfill prophecies of him (but see Isa. 53!). Jews believe Jesus was one of many martyrs and that he was at most a great teacher of righteousness.

Yeshua is the original Hebrew given name for Jesus of Nazareth. The Hebrew *Yeshua* is translated as "Salvation" in English. See the connection between *thy Salvation* and *thy Yeshua* in Genesis 49:18 and Luke 2:29-30, scriptures which are not linked in the LDS Bible. *(More: page 46)*.

Jehovah: To a Jew, the Lord "Jehovah", is their one God. He is Heavenly Father. To a Christian, Jehovah is Jesus Christ. When Jesus appeared to the Nephites in the Book of Mormon he explained he was **the God of Avraham, Isaac and Jacob** and that he had given the Israelites the Law. Jews do not know this.

Messiah, *Moshiach.* Anglicization of the Hebrew, *"Moshiach"* (anointed one), often referred to as *"Moshiach* ben David" (Messiah, son of David). *(Isa 11:2-5, Jer 23:5, 33:15, Hosea 3:4,5)* One of the prevalent theories of the Messiah's origin and purpose is that he will be a human man chosen by God to bring about the political and spiritual redemption of the Jewish people. *(See Isaiah 11:11-12, Jeremiah 23:8, 30:3, and Hosea 3:4-5)*

The word *"Moshiach"* does not mean "savior." The notion of an innocent, divine or semi-divine being who will sacrifice himself to save us from the consequences of our own sins is a purely Christian concept that has no basis in Jewish thought. This Christian concept has become so deeply ingrained in the English word "messiah" that it cannot be used to refer to the Jewish concept. *(More: page 46)*

Prophets and Prophecy

Jews believe prophets receive communication from God when in a quiet state, sleep or a trance. Moses was considered the chief of all prophets, though he received revelation while awake. Jews believe that if a prophet immerses himself totally in *Torah* study and good works he may receive messages from God, but there is no guarantee. Women, too, can be prophetesses; Sarah, Miriam, Devorah and Esther. In Deuteronomy 8:15 Jews are commanded to listen to prophets. If a prophet predicts a miracle in the name of God and it is correct in every aspect, he is believed, but if one aspect is incorrect, he is false. If he contradicts *Torah*, he is a false revelator. Anciently those considered by the Jews to be false prophets were stoned to death.

BYU Professor Emeritus Truman Madsen notes that "among the Jews it is affirmed that today there is no prophet nor gift of prophecy, no one designated or recognized as a high priest for the most sacred rites, and especially those of the sanctuary, no sacred fire, no present glory of the *Shekhinah*, no holy anointing, no Temple, no prevailing unity of *halakhic* rulings, or of ritual procedure, or of essential teaching... Joseph Smith announced that the return is underway." *From Chosenness: Implications and Extensions in Mormonism and Judaism" by Truman G. Madsen. (More: page 49)*

Tzedakah (Charity)

The Hebrew word for giving aid and assistance. Derived from a root word meaning righteousness, justice or fairness. Charity suggests a magnanimous offering, but *tzedakah* is the performance of a duty. In Judaism this is an obligation that must be fulfilled even by those in need. This assistance is equal to repentance and prayer, the three acts that gain forgiveness. Jews believe people should keep from being in need themselves, but if they are truly in need it is wrong for them not to declare it. Jews believe also in tithing 10% of their income after payment of taxes. Those on welfare are asked to give a smaller percentage. The lesser rewarded level of *tzedakah* is to give begrudgingly, the greatest is to enable the recipient to become self-sufficient.

Jewish Mysticism

In truth, the Israelites were given the preparatory gospel at Sinai. The original Mosaic Law was taught by God's prophets to the Israelites. D&C 84:26-27 tells us the gospel principles include repentance, baptism for remission of sin, and obedience to the law of carnal commandments. When the Israelites rejected this higher law, the lesser one was placed in its stead, the full gospel being withheld. Paul, in Galatians 3, taught that Mosaic Law was instituted to bring the Jews to Christ. *Torah* records richly reflect that preparation of eternal values, which the Savior wishes each person on the earth to grasp and to live fully.

In the symbols of Israelite worship, similitudes of Christ can be found everywhere. Sacrifices and offerings represent the very center of Mosaic Law. Perhaps the most significant symbol set is represented by the animal sacrifices performed in the original traveling Tabernacle and in the First and Second Temples. The themes were repentance and cleansing of sin. Blood of the sacrificed goat; ram or bull was sprinkled on the altar. Children were sprinkled with blood to cleanse them of sin. In each temple ceremony there was an offerer, an offering and the priesthood officiating. Following this ordinance, the offerer was deemed free of guilt for sins because they had been destroyed symbolically through the literal burning of a dead animal. Fire was the cleansing element.

How To Build a Bridge

Approach Jews from the hallmarks of their belief and cultural system. If you can gain their confidence, ask them about their heritage, their customs, their holidays. Invite them to ask you questions. When referring to Jesus Christ, use *Yeshua*. They must hear that *Yeshua* is the god of Avraham, Isaac and Jacob. You will have to pray mightily that the Holy Ghost will touch your contacts to effect change, because they will discern eventually that they're being faced with a *change of identity*. This is a Herculean, frightening task for a Jew, but of course one that must eventually be accomplished, for we know that "every knee must bend and every tongue confess that Jesus is the Christ".

Here are some dos and don'ts and other ideas to use.

Tips for Opening Dialogues

- Greet with a Hebrew greeting: "*Shalom aleichem*". (Repeat it when you leave.) Ask for their help if you don't know the correct pronunciation.

- The Jewish people have been proselytized by Christians for centuries. Many are reviled by it, and they hurriedly dismiss visitors whose message, book or badge mentions Jesus Christ.

- You might also say that you represent *Yeshua*, the God of Avraham, Isaac and Jacob. If they show confusion, be aware that many will think a "Church" has sent you, not the Lord (the God of Avraham, Isaac and Jacob).

- Take a few moments to get to know your Jewish neighbor. Kibbitz (talk) with them a while; find something to compliment or comment on.

- A Jewish person might be less intimidated if you say you are Mormon. Many Jewish people know and like LDS people.

- If you see a *mezuzah* (See Glossary) on the doorpost of a Jewish family's home, you may touch it (even say a prayer!). After all, men with the priesthood of God are truly rabbis.

- Be guided by the Spirit. Be aware that if you give a testimony of "Jesus Christ" at the door, you may have it closed in your face. If you testify of *Yeshua*, your prospect will be more apt to listen.

Show Interest

- As in any interfaith communication, start out with compliment of another's culture, faces, symbols, country, language, HOST culture. If you can use some Hebrew words of greeting, this may disarm them. If you cannot say these words correctly, ask for their help.

- Don't inquire much about your hosts' personal history. Your contact may be uneasy because you are Christian and a stranger. They have historical reasons to have fear.

- **Remember you are a guest in another culture.** Open your mind to things around you. Ask questions, show genuine interest, share some related knowledge from your own life. Ask about your host or hostess, forget about yourself.

- If you see a *mezuzah* on the doorframe, your contact will be an Orthodox or Conservative Jew. Ask about the *mezuzah*. Express interest and delight. When a comfortable contact is established, ask about their religion and be appreciative of it. Ask about their special holidays. You should already know about the next Jewish holiday coming up. *(See Major Jewish Holidays, page 60.)*

- You may be observed by other Jewish families while at your contact's door. Understand you may be asked to leave for this reason alone. Ask if you can return another time or meet them in another location.

- Put your contact at ease. Be informal, engage in conversation, be disarming, show genuine appreciation and interest. Be gentle, caring, non-pushy in your demeanor and presentation. Be polite and humble. Listen to what you are told, and work from that. Approach the Gospel carefully, without hurry or insistence.

The Value of the Doctrine and Covenants

The Doctrine and Covenants is a holy book. It has been *the* prime mover for many Jewish converts, including the author. It is direct revelation to a prophet of God; not a translation from some dubious source. It contains questions and answers, problems and solutions and inspired information about matters of mortal and eternal life.

Talmud is a collection of commentaries upon and insights into the *Torah*, or Pentateuch. Jews read *Talmud* for wisdom and instruction, but these commentaries are only the wisdom of sages and rabbis, and though core virtues of Mosaic Law are expressed at length, the work in general is filled with suppositions and false conclusions. Jewish converts have realized that the Doctrine and Covenants is superior to the *Talmud* in every way, and <u>it has been an important element of conversion to the Church</u>. One reason for this is that the Lord speaks to us in the first person much of the time; therefore, the book is a like a personal message from our Savior!

It is important to let your Jewish investigator know of this book so he may discover that the Doctrine and Covenants contain revelations to mankind from the only Begotten Son of God and <u>contains only perfect doctrine</u>. The *Talmud*, written by men through the centuries who at times have been inspired, cannot be compared with the proclamation that the Doctrine and Covenants is a divine and inspired collection. Jewish contacts need to be exposed to the scope of subject matter in the doctrinal "essays". Read the revelatory and testamentary material contained therein, and realize the timeliness of these proclamations of instruction is a factor in knowing the Church of Jesus Christ of Latter-day Saints is their true home.

Let your Jewish contact read the introductory paragraphs to the work itself, especially those relating the list of topics, as well as the testimonies of the twelve apostles.

Relevant Ideas for Sharing

If you are able to make good contact, **teach to the similarities.** You might begin with the 10th Article of Faith. Be aware that in many ways there is little breach between Judaism and Christianity as it was <u>originally</u> taught. Remember that the Savior was a Jew. In the Second Temple he read from *Torah* scrolls. Latter-day Saints have been given in good part the restoration of ancient Hebrew beliefs. Mention similarities in faith, reading scriptures, morality, fasting, honoring life and *mitzvots* (commandments, also charity), repentance, Sabbath practices, the ending of blood sacrifice with an infinite atonement. Mention that the "mercy seat" in the ancient tabernacle in the desert during the Exodus, as well as in Solomon's and Herod's temples, represented the atoning sacrifice that was to be given when *Yeshua* ministered. <u>If you use the terms *Yeshua* and Jehovah instead of Jesus Christ; your contact will be more comfortable with those words.</u>

The *Yom Kippur* service, the Day of Atonement, is based upon repentance. Explain how the Savior is involved in this process through his atoning sacrifice and review the steps of repentance taught by the Church. Repentance literally means "re-punish" in Latin. To repent is to rethink the situation and change direction. "Turn" in Hebrew is *shuvah*. The root *shuv*, means to "turn back".

Explain how **the Articles of Faith are a fundamental support of the principles of Judaism** as are the 13 principles outlined in Maimonides' work which Orthodox Jews support *(see The 13 Principles of Faith)*.

Mention **ancient writings of Judaism (*Kaballah*) which talk about souls needing to progress to higher elevations**: "from strength to strength" (Also see Psalm 84). What else can be the reason for the resurrection of the dead? Resurrection of the dead is taught in *Torah* study:Mention the *Yahrzeit* prayers for the dead who, to a Jew, are ascending yearly toward God. Compare with the three levels of glory as taught by Paul in the New Testament.

Mystical Judaism speaks of a spiritual world, *Olam Habriyah*, through which all spirits must pass before they can descend to the physical world. Compare with LDS belief in a premortal existence. Explain how this corresponds to the purpose of eternal progression. You might explain further:

- that death is a temporary phenomenon and that body and spirit will be reunited.

- how LDS temples further the work through the restoration of ancient temple ordinances.

- that LDS temples are essentially re-creations of Solomon's and Herod's temples.

The scapegoat in ancient *Yom Kippur* services was a symbol of casting sin upon an intercessor whose resulting death served as atonement.Explain that **when Jews made repentance through the sacrifices of animals, the blood spilled upon the altar was in similitude of the blood of Christ** who was the infinite sacrifice. Mention the ancient Jewish priesthood duties of helping people to repent through these sacrifices, and how this is comparable to priesthood duties today. Book of Mormon prophet Abinidi explained the law of performances and ordinances and types of things to come. These scripture will help to clarify this principle *(Mos 13:30-33, 16:14-15)*.

Explain that **all the Hebrew prophets described Jesus** (*Yeshua*), his birth, ministry sacrifice and resurrection. Jews think of someone akin to Bruce R. McConkie's *Millenial Messiah* as the *Moshiach* they expected. They should be told that he came first as a **mortal** Messiah to all people to perform the atonement. He has a Church upon the earth today. He will return to Jerusalem as a mortal and **will** come as the conquering **millennial** *Moshiach.* He will save the Jewish people from destruction by their enemies and they will know and accept him in a day. He will fulfill the remaining three Feasts of Israel *(see Major Jewish Holidays, page 60)*, a new temple will be built in Jerusalem and the Melchizedek priesthood will be bestowed. Jewish tribal lineage will be reclaimed at that time.

Yeshua came to fulfill ancient prophecy and covenants relating to the Avrahamic Covenant and the mission of the prophet Elijah, as well as Israelite prophetic revelations about *Yeshua* from *Torah*.

Location of *Moshiach*'s Birth	Micah 5:2
First Time of Coming Foretold	Gen 49:10, Isa. 9:6
Death Foretold	Psalms 22:1, 18, Zach 11:12, 12:10, 13:6
Called Out of Egypt	Hosea 11:1
First Ministry of the Messiah	Isa. 41:6-8, 61:1,3, 53
Resurrection of Men	Isa. 26:16-17
Through Judah-Chief Ruler	Gen 18:18, 22:18, 1 Chron 5:2
Kingdom Through David	2 Sam 76:12-17, 1 Chron 17:11-15
Prophecies Fulfilled	Rev 19:16, Zech 14:9
Second Coming	Dan 7:13-14, Mal 3:1-6, Rev 6:15-17, Zech 12:6-10
The Latter Days	Job 19:25-27
LORD Will Judge People	Mal 3:1-6, 4:1, Isa. 24:20-23

Tell of Book of Mormon prophecies of Jesus' ministry. A point of information is that members of the families of Judah, Levi, Joseph and the other sons of Jacob were in slavery in Egypt and they all made the trek across the desert to unite as a nation of Israel. Members of these families also came across the ocean with Lehi from Jerusalem around 600 B.C.

Nephi foresaw the mission, scattering, trials and destiny of the Jewish people. *(1Ne 15:12-18, 13:42, 2Ne 27:1, Mormon 7:8)*

Lehi was a descendant of Manasseh, son of Joseph who was sold into Egypt. The Assyrians captured members of Ephraim and Manasseh in 721 B.C. Others of these two families who were taken to Jerusalem in 941 B.C. may have included the forefathers of Lehi and Ishmael. There is a lot of attention paid to desert life in the Book of Mormon, 1 Nephi. This cultural similarity to Lehi's descriptions of the Jerusalem area is not coincidental. An excellent book is *Discovering Lehi, New Evidence of Lehi and Nephi in Arabia,* by Lynn M. Hilton and Hope A. Hilton, Cedar Fort, 1996.

There are 433 verses from Isaiah in the Book of Mormon. These are on the Small Plates of Nephi. The Plates of Brass brought by the people of Lehi from Jerusalem in 600 B.C. contained the five books of Moses (*Torah*), a record of the Jews from their beginning to the reign of King Zedekiah, Judah's king, as well as Lehi's genealogy and various prophetic writings.

The name Lehi relates to the Hebrew word meaning to/for life, "(*l'chai*)". Melek, the Nephite land, is a Hebrew word meaning "king". Mosiah, MoSHEah (מוסיה), means servant or helper, and is the theme of King Benjamin's Sukkot discourse. Mosiah may have the root word "Moses". The "iah" ending is distinctly characteristic of Hebraic names. There are other names in the Book of Mormon reminiscent of Hebrew words.

Jewish contacts may be interested in the trek of Lehi to America as well as the historical, linguistic and genealogical value of the Brass Plates to the people of America. Tell them how the Nephite and Lamanite populations practiced the Law of Moses (*Mosheh*=child, son).

An important point concerning Lehi's trail: People normally dream about images that are familiar, such as family members, our home, work, locations in our environment. But the images in Lehi's dream were images familiar to the desert world in which Lehi was wandering. The Tree-of-Life tradition is known in many cultures around the world, particularly from the Near East to Greece to India and also in Central America. Jewish mysticism also has a tree of life construct in Jewish mystical literature that consists in part of a theory of the ways in which they believe God manifests His nature and purpose to mankind.

This Tree of Life tradition usually included a tree as a symbol, often white or with white fruit, also mentioning springs or a pool of water, a path leading to the tree and sometimes people under the tree. The Egyptians had an elaborate Tree-Of-Life literature. These literatures are two that Lehi may have been familiar with and which may have influenced his dream.

This is another evidence verifying the fact that the Book of Mormon is of Semitic origin and not written by an American in the 19th Century. Joseph Smith could not have dreamed of a Arabic desert environment. He had no knowledge of those things; he had read no books about them. He gained that knowledge through revelation. He translated the Golden Plates through the gift and power of God.

In 1 Nephi 8:4-8: **Lone traveler Lehi sees "a dark and dreary waste."** He "traveled for the space of many hours in darkness." These images are common in Arabic lyric poetry and have been found as inscriptions scratched on rocks in the Arabian desert. The standard nightmare of the Arab is traveling long distances through dark and dreary wastes. Only one who had actually seen those things could have dreamed them; only one who had been haunted by those fears and frightened by those situations could express them as Lehi did.

The line of descent of the Savior is traceable through seven dispensations: **Adam** (4000 B.C.) to Seth, Enos, Cainan, Mahalaleel, Jared, **Enoch**, Methuselah, Lamech, **Noah** (2944 B.C.), Shem, Arphaxad, Salah, Eber, Peleg, Reu, Serug, Nahor, Terah, **Avraham** (1992 B.C.), Isaac, Jacob, **Judah**, **David**, Jechonias, **Jesus** (approx. 7 B.C.) See 2 Ne 19:7 and Isa. 9:7.

The message is: there is no end to the throne of David. The line of descent of the Prophet Joseph Smith is linked to Joseph of the Coat of Many Colors. He was a type and shadow of the Savior and of latter day prophecies.

Holy documents are hid up to preserve their purity until it is time for them to come forth. Buried plates with ancient writings were discovered in ancient Israel in 1950, covered with Semitic characters pressed into the plates by an instrument, from the late Hittite period (Lehi's time). Also sheets with Hebrew-Aramaic writings from A.D. 200 mention a god of Israel, and the Dead Sea Scrolls also contain much information about early Israel. These were wrapped and hidden in earthenware jars in a manner prescribed to Moses.

In the Book of Mormon, Alma speaks about white-robed figures, sanctified high priests of God. He appeals to people to "keep your garments spotless, that ye may at last be brought to sit down with Abraham, Isaac and Jacob and the holy prophets" (Alma 7:25,13:11-12.) He discourses on subjects dear to *Talmudic* scholars: life beyond the grave, the Messiah, the importance of a Savior. This is known in Judaism as a "vertical prophetic tradition". (*The Prophetic Book of Mormon, Hugh Nibley.*)

Tell your Jewish contacts about **Orson Hyde's visit to Jerusalem in 1841 and his prayer upon the Mount of Olives.** (*See page 97 for a portion of his prayer*). In addition, President Lorenzo Snow dedicated Jerusalem for the return of the Jewish people in the 1870's. (*Church History, B.H. Roberts, vol 2*)

Elijah's return is associated with the Passover. He did return to the Kirtland Temple on the second day of *Pesach* (Passover) which was also Easter Sunday, 16 *Nisan*, 3 April, 1836. First the Savior appeared, then Elias, then Elijah. Moses restored the "keys of the gathering of Israel" *(D&C 110:11)*, Elias committed the dispensation of the Gospel of Avraham, saying that "in us and our seed all generations after us should be blessed" *(D&C 110:12)*, and Elijah restored "the power to hold the key of the revelations, ordinances, oracles, powers and endowments of the fullness of the Melchizedek Priesthood and of the kingdom of God on the earth, etc."

The Book of Mormon is full of Hebraisms and Hebraic literary devices, such as *Chiasmus*, a set of parallels framed on a structure which folds upon itself, revealing a central focus. *(See 1Ne 10:12-14, 2Ne 25:47, and the section on Character Of Hebrew Writing; page 2)*. The richness of Jewish scripture is enhanced in LDS scripture. Alma 36 is a prime example of all chiastic structures.

From Joseph Smith's *Lectures On Faith*, explain what faith is and the object on which it rests (Heavenly Father), His being and attributes, the effects that flow from faith, how a person works from faith, etc. Many of these treatments are supported by scriptural citations from Isaiah and the other *Torah* prophets. *(See LDS Scriptural Citations.)*

Talmud writings include free will issues. **The Pharisees** (separatists) believed all people have agency. They also believed in the **resurrection of the dead and the reward of everlasting life that would be the lot of the righteous.** Most accepted the popular hope for a Messiah from the line of David.

A Survey: What Do Jews Really Know

A Church survey conducted during the 1970's concluded the following about mainstream modern-day Jews.

- Many Jewish people know very little about their own Jewish identity or the difference between the terms Jews, Israelites, or Hebrews.

- Many don't know the origins of their traditions, the nature or personality of God, or Messianic literature, expectations or purposes. The concepts they do embrace are generally incorrect.

- Jews know little about the meaning or tradition of priesthood. The rabbi, Jewish spiritual leader, is not ordained. He is appointed by the congregation and can be dismissed by them.

- Jews have a small knowledge of the prophet Isaiah and all other prophets. Many congregations do not tithe, but many give to aid in the building and preservation of their synagogue and schools.

- Jewish religious training basically prepares children for their rites of passage ceremonies (*Bar* and *Bat Mitzvahs* and confirmations). They are taught correct observances of Jewish holidays and traditions but little insight into *Talmudic* knowledge or history is offered.

- Many Jews do not know Hebrew or Yiddish.

- Jews do not believe Jesus Christ is their Mashiach (Messiah). They reject and revile the idea that he came to teach Messianic scriptures to the Jews and that he was their "king".Because of many omissions and corruptions to worship practices that have occurred in modern times, the Jewish people have been left with no saving ordinances. This is not a criticism, but a deeply disturbing fact. They don't know what a *saving* ordinance is, or that they must have it to partake of the glory that is available to all of us.

- We understand that we shall all be changed at the Second Coming of Christ and that the dead in Christ shall rise first. Graves are like buds, they will open and the fruit of death shall be immortality. When the Savior ministered to the Hebrews, he taught that as *he* was resurrected from the grave, *they* would conquer death, but if they do not accept Christ and his Church, they are unaware of further opportunities: eternal life, bonding for eternity to spouse and children, family continuance and eternal progression culminating with the inheritance of all things our Heavenly Father possesses.

The following passages in the Hebrew scriptures—in the Five Books of Moses (Pentateuch)—are those that Jews consider to be messianic in nature or relating to the end of days. These are the ones we Saints rely upon in developing our messianic concept:

Lineage, Divine Birth, Youth	
Genesis 49:9,10	Of the tribe of Judah
Psalms 2:7	The Father acknowledges him to be His Son
Isaiah 7:14; 9:16-7	Born of a virgin, place of birth, lineage of David
Isaiah 11:1,10; 53:2; 60:6	Lineage, grow as plant, the Magi (Matt 2:11)
Jeremiah 23:5,6	Of the house of David
Jeremiah 31:15, 33:15	Massacre of innocents, lineage (Matt 2:18)
Daniel 3:25; 7:13	References to the Son of God
Hosea 11:1	Taken for refuge into Egypt (Matt 2:15)
Micah 5:2,3	Relation to God, of tribe of Judah, born in Bethlehem
Mortal Ministry	
Deut 18:15-19	Advent, prophet
Psalms 8:2; 35:11	Triumphant entry, condemnation
Psalms 41:9; 45:1-17	Betrayal by friend, characteristics of life and work
Psalms 56:1-6; 69:8-9	Presence of enemies, disbelief of brethren, temple cleansing
Psalms 71:10-11; 72:1-20	Plots against Christ, his life and work
Psalms 78:2; 110:1-4	Teaching, parables, his life and work
Psalms 118:22-23, 26	Rejected of men, acclamations on; entry in Jerusalem

Proverbs 8:32-36	His teachings
Isaiah 6:9-10; 8:14	Rejected teachings, rejected of men to Jews
Isaiah 9:1; 11:1-3; 28:16	Place of ministry, life and work, cornerstone
Isaiah 40:3; 9-11; 42:1-5	Herald goes before him, time of Advent, persecution
Isaiah 49:7; 50:4-9; 52:13-15	Persecution, his life and work
Isaiah 53:1-3; 61:1-2	His life and work, teachings
Jeremiah 7:11	Desecration and cleansing of temple
Zechariah 9:9; 11:12-13	Triumphal entry to Jerusalem, betrayal
Exodus 12:1-14; 46	Lamb of God, bones not broken
Leviticus 16:7-22	Sin offering in behalf of people
Numbers 21:6-9	Brass serpent lifted on pole to save people
Job 19:25	Reference to Redeemer
Psalms 22:1-19; 31:4-5	Suffering and crucifixion
Psalms 34:20; 35:11; 41:9	No bone broken, condemnation, betrayal
Psalms 69:9,21; 109:21-26`	Mocked, his sufferings
Psalms 118:22,23	Rejected of men
Isaiah 8:14,15; 49:7-8	Rejected of men, stumbling stone, mediator
Isaiah 52:3, 4-12; 59:16	Suffering, atonement, death, intercessor provided
Isaiah 63:3	Blood of others upon him
Daniel 9:24-26	Cut off, vicarious sacrifice
Hosea 13:4,14	Savior, Redeemer and Ransomer
Zechariah 11:12,13	Betrayal by friend and disciple
Zechariah 12:10; 13:6-7	Pierced, betrayed

Resurrection, Triumph and Divinity

Genesis 1:1	Called the Word of God (Ps 33:6, Jn 1:1-14)
2 Samuel 7:12	King of Israel
Job 19:25	To stand upon the earth
Psalms 2:6-8; 8:4-6	Exaltation, Son of Man, supremacy
Psalms 16:10-11; 17:15	Resurrection
Psalms 45:17; 56:13; 68:18	Name eternal, resurrection, ascension, triumph
Psalms 72:17; 89:27; 110:1-3	Name eternal, firstborn, King of Kings, exaltation
Psalms 110:4-7; 118: 17-19	Resurrection and triumph
Proverbs 8:22-31	Foreordination and divinity
Isaiah 9:6-7; 11:2-5	Mighty God, kingdom, supremacy
Isaiah 45:23; 53:10; 61: 1-3	Ultimate universal acceptance, immortality, kindness, power
Daniel 7:13-14	Son of man to have everlasting dominyan
Hosea 13:14	To destroy death
Jonah 1:17	Raised on third day (Matt 16:4)
Malachi 4:1-2	Second Advent foretold

Additional Scriptures

Isaiah 2, 11, 42; 59:20	Latter-day temples and gathering of Israel
Jeremiah 23, 30, 33; 48:47; 49:39	Remnants of Israel gathered in last days
Ezekiel 38:16	The war of Gog and Magog
Hosea 3:4-3:5	Israel will seek the Lord and return to him in last days
Micah 4	Latter-day temple built for Israel, millennial reign begins
Zephaniah 3:9	Men shall have a pure language, the Second Coming
Zechariah 14:9	Lord shall be king over whole earth, one Lord, one name.
Daniel 10:14	Vision of what will befall Israel in latter days.

Source: The Life and Teachings of Jesus and His Apostles Course Manual, 2nd Edition, The Church of Jesus Christ of Latter-day Saints, 1979, SLC, Utah.

Differences between Judaism and LDS

Monotheism	**Jewish**	-
Belief in *Torah* as final arbiter of all of life's rules, rewards, the garment of life	**Jewish**	-
Method of prayer is ritualistic. Prayers are recited exactly as written	**Jewish**	-
Open canon, not a finalized religion or culture	**Jewish**	**LDS**
Knowledge that families of Joseph are to bring Judah into the LDS church		**LDS**
Interest in or understanding of Jesus the Christ	-	**LDS**
The Messiah has arrived and is Jesus Christ	-	**LDS**
Atonement of Savior has been accomplished	-	**LDS**
The Messiah put on mortality through Mary, immortality through God		**LDS**
Personal savior recognized as Jesus. Prayers offered in Jesus' name	-	**LDS**
Personal prayers taught and encouraged		**LDS**
Belief in modern revelation or promptings	-	**LDS**
Modern prophets lead restored Church of Jesus Christ	-	**LDS**
Priesthood restoration has been accomplished	-	**LDS**
Lay leaders, unpaid clergy	-	**LDS**
Literal belief in life after death for the soul of man	-	**LDS**
Saving ordinances	-	**LDS**
Acknowledgement of a modern temple	-	**LDS**
Ordinance work for dead (Elijah's return) has been restored	-	**LDS**
Holy Ghost part of basic liturgy, part of the Godhead	-	**LDS**
Concerned with **only** true principles	-	**LDS**
Complete, true understanding of the Fall of Man through Adam and Eve	-	**LDS**

Similarities between Judaism and LDS

Members of the twelve families of Israel	**Both**
Under the Avrahamic Covenant, both called Covenant Israel because the blood of Israel is in their veins	**Both**
Worship the same Heavenly Father	**Both**
Belief in the Ten Commandments as given to Moses	**Both**
Belief in a kingdom of priests and a holy nation	**Both**
Ancient holders of holy priesthoods	**Both**
Belief in angels, holy and unholy visitations	**Both**
Belief in the idea and reality of a Messianic figure	**Both**
Belief in sacrifice as atonement for sin	**Both**
Belief in Old Testament (*Torah*) prophets, revelations from God	**Both**
Belief the Mashiach will be a descendant of Davidic line	**Both**
Belief in temples. The synagogue is a type of temple	**Both**
Belief in prayer, sacred religious rituals and consecrated behaviors	**Both**
Practice a form of baptism, anointing, laying on of hands	**Both**
Administer "new" names to those completing ordinances	**Both**
Belief in giving aid, monetary assistance and other charity to those in need	**Both**
Belief in a pre-mortal life and an afterlife	**Both**
LDS believe Elijah has returned. Jews believe he will return on the Passover	**Both**
Do not see death as tragedy	**Both**
Belief in the eventual redemption of the dead	**Both**
Believe in eventual resurrection of the dead	**Both**
Belief in the End Days theories that will bring peace and joy	**Both**
Congregations led by appointed representatives	**Both**
Believe in living basic Mosaic law of chastity, honesty, charity, Sabbath observance	**Both**
Crosses not used as symbols in either church or synagogue	**Both**
Both religions acknowledge Jesus as a teacher of righteousness	**Both**

Both religions have strict dietary laws	**Both**
Jews and Mormons wear sacred garments under clothes, outer vestments	**Both**
General knowledge or interest in scripture learning, reading, quoting	**Both**
Members encouraged to study, learn and achieve	**Both**
Members are taught self-sufficiency	**Both**
Belief in family as essential to a happy, productive life, basis of society	**Both**
Belief in marrying inside the religion and culture	**Both**
Belief in an Adversary and his evil influences, Belief that good overcomes evil	**Both**
Acknowledgement of mysteries of creation beyond human knowledge	**Both**
Societies have undergone religious persecution, exodus, re-settlement for beliefs	**Both**
Belief that God will personally reign upon the earth (Jews: Elohim) (LDS: Christ)	**Connections**
Former and latter-day prophets have used the *Urim* and *Thummim*	**Connections**
The Jewish *Tanakh* scriptures have parallels and similarities to the LDS "quad" in subject matter, wisdom, purpose	**Connections**
LDS temple ordinances, symbols are based upon sacred Israelite rites and practices	**Connections**
Belief in revelation and prophecy available to anyone (Jews: rabbis exert powerful but limited influence	**Connections**
Church of Jesus Christ of Latter-day Saints based upon Mosaic Law as given to Moses	**Connections**
Jews know their Messiah will come. He will be a Jew. LDS know that the Savior has come and is Jesus Christ	**Connections**
Messianic Jews already know that Jesus is the Christ. They call him *Yeshua*	**Connections**
Book of Mormon prophets are descendents of Hebrew prophets, although the Jewish people are as yet unaware of it	**Connections**
Book of Mormon prophets as well as Hebrew prophets have received revelations about the gathering in these last days of the 10 lost tribes and their eventual return to Israel	**Connections**

Circumcision practiced. **Jews**: a covenant with God and the mark of their identity. **LDS**: having a broken heart and a contrite spirit	**Connections**
Mormon prophets pray for the redemption of Israel and the gathering of Israel to the lands of their inheritance. Jews pray for peace and redemption of Israel to Jerusalem	**Connections**

Two additional connections between Jews and the Restoration of the Gospel:

(1) The Golden Plates were delivered by the angel Moroni to Joseph Smith on *Rosh Hashonah*, September 22, 1827, when Jews all over the world were praying for the restoration of the *brit,* meaning covenant.

(2) Following the restoration of the Gospel on *Passover*, April 3, 1836, the Lord *Yeshua* appeared in vision to the Prophet Joseph Smith and Oliver Cowdery in the Kirtland, Ohio temple.

Worship and Religious Practices

Shabbat (Sabbath)

The Sabbath (*Shabbat*) is a hallmark of Jewish belief and practice. **It is the most important ritual observance in Judaism**, also one of the best known and least understood of all Jewish observances. Like all Jewish days, it begins at sunset *(See Genesis 1)* every Friday and lasts 24 hours to sunset on Saturday. Jews believe *Shabbat* is a precious gift from God, a day of great joy eagerly awaited throughout the week, when we set aside all of our weekday concerns and devote ourselves to higher pursuits. In Jewish literature, poetry and music, *Shabbat* is described as a bride or queen, as in the popular *Shabbat* hymn *L'cha Dodi Likrat Kallah* (Come, my beloved, to meet the [Sabbath] Bride). It is said "More than Israel has kept *Shabbat*; *Shabbat* has kept Israel."

Shabbat is the only ritual observance instituted in the Ten Commandments. It is also the most important special day. *Shabbat* is primarily a day of rest and spiritual enrichment. The word "*Shabbat*" means to cease or to rest. *Shabbat* is not specifically a day of prayer, though Jews do spend a substantial amount of time in synagogue praying. On *Shabbat*, they eat more elaborately and in a more leisurely fashion. The major divisions of Judaism celebrate the Sabbath with varying degrees of ritualism. In general, Jewry should experience the joy of union of God and mankind who is in exile on this earth. The King and Bride come together on Sabbath; harsh judgment is abandoned and all things taste of the joys of Eden. The banquet on the Sabbath night is in honor of the *Sheckinah*. This is her wedding feast. The banquet next noon is in honor of the Holy, Ancient One and the final meal just before sunset honors the King who sits in judgment.

Jews are commanded to remember *Shabbat* *(Ex 20:11)*. By resting on the seventh day and sanctifying it, Jews remember and acknowledge that God is the creator of heaven and earth and all living things. They also emulate the divine example by refraining from work on the seventh day. *(More: page 52)*

Priesthood

Cohen (sing.), *Kohanim* (pl.). The Aaronic priesthood was conferred upon Aaron and his seed throughout all generations. It holds the keys (responsibilities) to the temporal salvation of mankind and is concerned principally with repentance and baptism. The *Kohanim* were the direct descendents of Aaron, brother of Moses. David's sons were called *Kohanim (see 2 Sam 8:18 and 1 Chr. 18:17)*, generally translated as "priests" in *Torah*. Under the lesser priesthood, only men from the tribe of Levi were authorized to offer sacrifice to the Lord for the children of Israel or to preside as High Priest of the Levitical order (a descendent of Aaron within the tribe of Levi), though exceptions were made *(See 2 Sam 6)*. The function of the Levitical order is to serve the Aaronic priests in their duties. Not all Levites were *kohanim,* but the entire tribe of Levi was set aside to perform certain duties in connection with the Temple.

The Lord chose the tribe of Levi to assist Aaron in the priestly functions, the special duties of the Levites being to keep the instruments and attend to the service of the tabernacle. The Levites were to take the place of the firstborn throughout the tribes because the Lord claimed for His service from the time of the last dread plague in Egypt, whereby the firstborn in every Egyptian house was slain while the eldest in every Israelite house was hallowed and spared.

"The Lesser, or Aaronic Priesthood, was instituted when Israel was in the wilderness and that priesthood officiated in most of the affairs of the people of Israel until the restoration of the Melchizedek Priesthood by our Savior. However, the offices of the Aaronic Priesthood were not discarded in the Church in the day of the apostles, and have been continued in the Dispensation of the Fulness of Times. We have need for this priesthood now and will until the end of time and as long as temporal matters are essential to the progress of the Church. It is to be presumed that the higher priesthood will be held by all in the celestial kingdom when the earth is prepared for its exaltation." *From Answers to Gospel Questions, Joseph Fielding*

Smith, 5 vols. *[Salt Lake City: Deseret Book Co., 1957-1966], 1: 118.* **(More: page 52)**

Prayer

Observant Jews are constantly reminded of God's presence and of their relationship with God because they are continually praying to Him. Most prayers are ritualized and uttered exactly the same way each time. Observant Jews believe their first thought in the morning is a prayer thanking God for returning their souls to them. There are prayers to be recited before enjoying any material pleasure, such as eating or wearing new clothes; prayers to recite before performing any *mitzvah* (commandment), such as washing hands or lighting candles; prayers to recite upon seeing anything unusual, such as a rainbow, or the site of a great tragedy; prayers to recite whenever some good or bad thing happens; and prayers to recite before going to bed at night. All of these prayers are in addition to *saying* formal prayer at services, which are performed three times a day every weekday and at additional times during Shabbat and during festivals. The *Talmud* states that it is permissible to pray in any language that you can understand; however, traditional Judaism has always stressed the importance of praying in Hebrew. Traditional Judaism does not emphasize divine intervention through prayer or teach individual, personal communication with God, so many Jews do not know how to pray in this way!

Minyan – Prayer Circle

A wonderful principle of Jewish unity can be sensed in the repeated prayers said when a prayer circle of ten Jewish men is formed in Jewish ritual. "The rabbis placed great emphasis on the relationship of the individual to the community during prayer. Almost all prayer was written in the first person plural - "Forgive us," "Teach us," "Bring us to our Land." Although private prayer was certainly permitted, the individual was urged to join a congregation *(minyan)* when he prays and to incorporate the needs of the *minyan* in his prayers." *(Encyclopedia Judaica Jr.)* This practice is reminiscent of temple and community worship in Latter-day Saint life as well. Communal prayer opens the worshiper to the needs of others; it lifts our minds out of the narrowness of self-interest.

Tabernacles, temples

Torah speaks of the tabernacle and the temples. What is a temple but a palace? It is a palace where God walks, and where the Messiah visits the earth. It is a holy place. The book of Exodus invites us to the tabernacle. There are interesting facts associated with these holy places. The ancient tabernacle erected in the desert was a house where, as it says in D&C

109:15, every needful thing could be found. Moses received the instructions to build it when he spoke with our Lord on Mt. Sinai.

The temple is our salvation, it is literally life giving, life binding. It is where the unutterable name of God can be uttered. It is where sin is delivered up and atoned for, the final arbiter of a moral life, where Jews were cleansed of violation and found hope to go on. The Jews fitted their temple into their faith for they knew that the presence of the name of God alone in the Holy of Holies generated a powerful divine radiation called the *Sheckinah*, which was so powerful it would destroy any unauthorized person who approached that room.

LDS know the temple as much, much more. It is the central binding agent and the holy meeting place of mankind with God upon the earth because the LDS temples are where the Avrahamic Covenant is restored to its righteous heirs. *(More: page 53)*

Circumcision (brit milah) (or covenant cut)

This is the surgical removal of the foreskin of the penis of a male when he is eight days old through this ordinance. This law was given to the Jews in Gen 17:10-14. It represents an everlasting covenant between Deity and Avraham that the gospel and eternal opportunities were given to Avraham's descendents: circumcision was initially to be practiced by the chosen seed to identify and distinguish them until the *Moshiach* comes. Circumcision is performed by a *mohel* (*moyl*) who specializes in this duty. He is not usually a rabbi.

Bar Mitzvah, Bat Mitzvah

Bar Mitzvah literally means "son of the commandment". Under Jewish Law, children are not obligated to observe the commandments until they turn 12 (girls) or 13 (boys). *The Bar Mitzvah* ceremony for boys formally marks the assumption of that obligation; it is a rite of passage. At this ceremony, rights and obligations are conferred.

Girls have graduations equivalent to a *Bar Mitzvah*, called *Bas* or *Bat Mitzvah* (daughter of the commandment) and are accorded the respect of the elders.

The *Bar Mitzvah*ed youth are given their adult standing and can take part in religious rituals. They read *Torah* portions during *Shabbat* services, may testify before a religious court, and may make binding contracts and marry. They are expected to study *Torah* throughout their lives.

This achievement is very important. When invited, it is appropriate for LDS to attend these services. Congratulatory remarks are in order.

Age: While age 13 is the proper age for fulfillment of the Commandments, age 18 is the proper time for marriage and age 20 is the time for earning a livelihood. Elsewhere in *Talmud*, the proper age for marriage is said to be between ages 16-24.

Kosher Laws

The Jewish law of *kashrut* states what animals and foods are unclean and unholy and should not be eaten by a Jew. The most obvious idea behind *kashrut* is self-control and discipline. Jewish tradition allows use of animals as food and clothing; however, Jews are not supposed to rejoice in this or to make a sport of it. Some of the laws of *kashrut* are designed to prevent from becoming callous and cruel and to discourage hunting as a form of recreation or sustenance. To "keep kosher" is to observe strict rules regarding which foods are proscribed or permitted, when to eat what and when to abstain, the order of preparation, the cooking and the serving of food. *(Gen 9:4)* *(More: page 55)*

Jewish Congregations: Summary

Judaism is concerned more with actions than beliefs. Focus is on relationships and obligations between God and mankind, God and Israel, between mankind and his brethren.

Orthodox congregations believe there are absolute, unchanging laws from God. **Conservatives** believe there are laws from God that change and evolve over time. **Reform** and **Reconstructionist** Jews believe there are specific guidelines for all behavior which you can choose whether or not to follow. Reconstructionists are interspersed throughout liberal congregations. **Chasidism** emphasizes joy in prayer, encouraging song and dance as a medium through which to come to God and receive His blessings.

Though most Jews do not have any theological objections to praying in the synagogues of other movements, liberal services are not "rabbinic" enough for traditional Jews, and traditional services are too long, too conservative and often basically incomprehensible to liberal Jews (Orthodox services are primarily, if not exclusively, in Hebrew). Some Orthodox will not attend liberal services because of the mixed gender seating arrangements and because the liberal prayer book has omitted many traditional prayers.

Services in Reform, Conservative, and Orthodox synagogues have substantial differences in length, language, and choice of reading materials, but the overall structure is similar. *(More: page 56)*

Leadership in Synagogue

Rabbi, **Rebbe** A rabbi is not a priest. He has no more authority to perform rituals than any other adult male member of the Jewish community. A rabbi conducts services and is a spiritual leader, a teacher and guide to his synagogue and community. He will have education in Jewish law and tradition. He completes a course of study and receives a document (*semikhah)* confirming his authority to make decisions for his flock. He is paid by his congregation.

Chazzan (Cantor-Singer) A *chazzan* is the person who leads the congregation in prayer. Any person with good moral character and thorough knowledge of the prayers and melodies can lead the prayer services, and in many synagogues members of the community take this role. In smaller congregations, the rabbi often serves also as *chazzan*. Music plays a large role in Jewish religious services, so larger congregations usually hire a professional *chazzan*. Professional *chazzan*s are ordained clergy and paid for their services by the congregation. They can perform many of the pastoral duties of their community, in partnership with the rabbi. *(More: page 59)*

Major Expressions of Judaism

Mitzvah – Mitzvots (plural). *Mitzvots* are divine commandments, sometimes interpreted as good deeds. Judaism is focused on life and how to live it, not on the question of how to get into heaven. Jews perform the *mitzvah* because it is a privilege and a sacred obligation to do so. They perform out of a sense of love and duty, not a desire to get something in return. They are of various kinds; positive performance (charity), negative resolve (not sinning), between man and God (fasting, etc.), between man and man (honoring obligations), those that specify duties required of rabbis and those that honor suffering (inescapable burdens). These must be done with a joyful heart.

Terminology: God

In the Hebrew Bible, the word for "God" is written in four ways:

Elohim (אלהים) is translated as God (Heavenly Father). It is a plural of Eloah, from the Chaldean root El, meaning strength, mighty, the Almighty. In Exodus 6:2 we learn that the pre-Mosaic religion was an *El* religion, and that God appeared unto Avraham, Isaac and Jacob as *El Shaddai* (Almighty, from Babylonian *shaddu* (mountain).

Adonai (אדני) My Lord God, meaning my YHVH. Pronounced AH-**DO**-NOY; often used as *Adonaijah* (ad*on i jah*). Note that the "jah" has *Yahweh* in its Hebrew formation.

Yahveh, Yahweh (יהוה) Sometimes written as JHVH, the Tetragrammaton, the four-letter symbol that is translated as Lord (the god of Avraham, Isaac and Jacob). Anciently, scribes deliberately added incorrect vowel points to make the word unpronounceable. When combined with Elohim, the phrase, seen as **יהוה,** is translated as "Lord God". The Orthodox Jew never pronounces the name of God. It is sacred and must not be repeated or said in vain *(Ex 20:7, Lev 24:11)*. When the word is come upon in the Hebrew bible, it is pronounced "Adonai". The most popular transliteration is Jehovah.

Adonai **Elohenu (אלהינו)** My Lord our God. Pronounced AH-Do-Noy ElO-**HEY**-NEW.

Major Jewish Holidays

Work is not permitted on *Rosh Hashonah, Yom Kippur*, and some other holidays. Cooking, baking, transferring fire and carrying, all of which are forbidden on *Shabbat*, are permitted on holidays. All Jewish holidays begin the evening before the date specified. This is because a Jewish "day" begins and ends at sunset, rather than at midnight *(See Genesis 1)*. *(More detail on all holidays: page 60)*

Passover: Feast of the Unleavened Bread

EX:12:12, Lev:23:5-8
- Celebration of deliverance from Egypt
- Communion and Crucifixion, the body of Christ and his burial

Pesach (Passover) begins on the 15th day of the Jewish month of *Nisan* and lasts eight days. Of all the Jewish holidays, *Pesach* is the one most commonly observed, even by otherwise non-observant Jews. It is the first of the three major festivals with both historical and agricultural significance (the other two are *Shavuot* and *Sukkot*. Agriculturally, it represents the beginning of the harvest season in Israel. The primary observances of *Pesach* are related to the Exodus from Egypt after generations of slavery. It refers to the fact that God "passed over" the houses of the Jews when he was slaying the firstborn of Egypt. In English, the holiday is known as Passover. *Pesach* is also the name of the sacrificial offering (a lamb) that was made in the Temple on this holiday. *(More: page 60)*

The Feast of Passover, *Pesach,* celebrates the deliverance of the Jews from Egypt, a cleansing, a move from bondage in the world toward freedom and Heaven. Christian symbolism understands Passover as a passage from death in the grave to deliverance from death and sin, and from our sin to perfection in Christ. Jewish women light the *Pesach* candles because they are the pure hope of the world, as Jesus is to Christianity.

The reading of the Passover Haggadah (*Haggadah shel Pesah*) means literally the narration of the Exodus story as recited at the *seder* service. This manual is comprised of selections from the Holy Scriptures, their expositions in Talmudic literature, prayers and benedictions, legends and hymns and a guide for the ritual of the ceremony. In the Book of Mormon, there is reference to the prophet Alma advising his sons, probably during a Passover *seder.* Helaman, Corianton and Shiblon are admonished to be righteous in keeping the commandments of God. *(Alma 36-42).* This Passover ritual is itself a commandment. *(Deut 6:20-24, Ex 13:14).*

Several points should be in the forefront of our minds while we celebrate the holiday of Passover.

- We remember the Savior, Jesus Christ, who is *Yeshua Mashiach.* He commanded us to do so.

- The Passover lamb is a type and shadow of *Yeshua* because he was without blemish, meaning spiritually pure *(1Pet 2:22).*

- The way the Passover lamb was killed symbolized *Yeshua's* death *(Ex 12:46).*

- The prophet Isaiah described the Messiah's sacrificial death *(Isa 53:7). (The author thanks Sandra Hawkins for these insights.)*

- But this performance was to be only a type and shadow of the infinite sacrifice and atonement of Jesus Christ. He was the offerer, the offering and the priest. *(The Law of the Offerings. Andrew Jukes, 1966, Kegel Publications)*

Feast of Trumpets - Rosh Hashonah

Rosh Hashanah occurs on the first and second days of *Tishri. Rosh Hashonah* looks toward fulfillment of peace and adjudication of all problems on earth. It is one of the two High Holy Days. The Hosanna Shout originated here. In this festival Jews celebrate their liberty from Egypt and slavery. It is a feast of deliverance. *Torah* is carried through the congregation. As the Israelites overcame their foes, so we may see this feast as a type and similitude of the Second Coming of Christ, when the Savior will come with a shout and the blowing of trumpets or *shofars* and the children of Israel will come from everywhere to join him in the vanquishing of the Adversary and the ushering in of Zion. God may use the ram's horn to deliver the trump sound of the Advent of the Savior. *(More: page 63)*

Yom Kippur, Day of Atonement

Yom Kippur, the second High Holy Day in Judaism is probably the most important holiday of the Jewish year. It occurs on the 10th day of *Tishri*. Many Jews who do not observe any other Jewish custom will refrain from work, dedicate a total fast and/or attend synagogue services on this day. The holiday is instituted in Leviticus 23:26 *et seq*.

DO NOT WISH JEWS A HAPPY HOLIDAY ON *YOM KIPPUR!*

Yom Kippur reminds the pious how Avraham was reprieved after offering his son in sacrifice. Very solemn, with anguish, it recapitulates the long history of violence and humiliation to which Jews have been subjected. Because they believe they must be forgiven by other men before they can ask forgiveness of God, they make it a priority to make up with those they have offended in any way during the preceding ten days. Once prayers begin, they continue from morning to sunset without interruption.

The primary feature of Yom Kippur is confession of sins. There are 56 categories and a prayer is required for each. Jews use "we", not "I" in asking for forgiveness because they share each other's burdens as well. *(More: page 34)*

Feast of Lights, Temple Rededication - Chanukah

Chanukah is probably one of the best known Jewish holidays, not because of any great religious significance, but because of its proximity to Christmas. Many non-Jews think of this holiday as the Jewish Christmas, adopting many of the Christmas customs, such as elaborate gift-giving and decoration. It is bitterly ironic that this holiday, which has its roots in a revolution against assimilation and the suppression of Jewish religion, has become the most assimilated, secular holiday on the Jewish calendar.

Prophesied Restoration

Israel is the promised ancestral and, according to latter-day scripture and revelation, the promised and future home of the Jews *(Isa. 11:11, 12, 29:14; D&C 103:13; Dedicatory Prayer of Orson Hyde, 1841)*. Israel was declared an independent state in May 1948. All Jews who go to Israel are accorded automatic citizenship if they can prove their birth heritage.

After the fall of Jerusalem around 586 B.C. a Hebrew prophet named Lehi (meaning to/for life) was commanded by God to build a boat and sail it with his family to the Americas where great civilizations of the Nephites and Lamanites (possibly also the Jaredites) were started. The Jaredite tribes also populated areas of America. They are some of the descendents of original Israelite families. Some modern American Indians are the remnant of these ancient peoples, whose true story is told in the Book of Mormon. This book, translated from golden plates by a modern-day prophet of the Restoration, Joseph Smith, gives information about their social, religious and spiritual history. The reformed Egyptian characters that the latter-day prophet translated into English became modified through time to form some of the Hebrew alphabet which was not in daily usage until Lehi's time, around 600 B.C.

Part 2: For Further Study

This section provides a more detailed study of matters relating to your Jewish friends. Some of the topics in this section are:

  The Jewish race and ethnic groups.

  Diasporas, Jewish People In Spiritual Diaspora

  Sacred Books of the Jews

  Basic Jewish beliefs

  Worship and Religious Practices

  Jewish Congregations

  Major Jewish Holidays

  Fulfilling the Law and Prophecies

  All Righteous Things Testify of Christ

For basic understanding (less detailed study), please start with Part 1. For reference material, see Part 3.

The Jewish Race

In the 1980s, the United States Supreme Court ruled that Jews are a race, at least for purposes of certain anti-discrimination laws. But modern Jews may not consider themselves racially connected, though the first Israelites of Avraham and Moses' time (circa 2000 B.C.) were descendents of nomadic Phoenician and Semitic tribes wandering in the Levant area that surrounds the Mediterranean Sea. Today these lands are under the jurisdiction of Jordan, Syria, Turkey, Greece and Egypt. Semites were of Caucasian stock formed from Phoenicians, Babylonian, Assyrian tribes and others of the eastern Mediterranean area. They claim descent from Avraham, Isaac and Jacob; they were the ancestors of the Hebrew people who were in the area of Israel during the time of the *Torah* writings.

Both Jews and Latter-day Saints know of the covenant between the patriarch Abraham (really Avraham) and Heavenly Father *(Genesis 12:2-3)*. Avram the Hebrew was promised by the Lord that his posterity would become a great nation and in him and his seed all the families of the earth would be blessed. Avram's name was changed to Avraham (father of many). Avraham's sons were Ishmael, father to the Arab nations, and Isaac (Yitzhak), whose sons were Esau and Jacob. Jacob's name was changed to Israel *(Gen 35:10)*. He had twelve sons from whom came the twelve families of Israel.

Ethnic Groups

There are two main ethnic groups of Jews to consider: *Ashkenazic* (Germanic) and *Sephardic* (Moorish or Spanish).

The **Ashkenazic.** Jews were originally located in Italy, France, Germany, Britain and eventually Eastern Europe. They established great centers of learning in Poland, the Ukraine and Russia. In addition to Hebrew, Ashkenazim speak *Yiddish*.

The **Sephardim** followed the advance of Islam, settling in North Africa, Spain and Portugal. They have spread to many South American countries since their dispersion in 1492 from Spain when King Ferdinand and Queen Isabella gave Jews the choice of being forcibly converted to Catholicism or leaving the country. The main *Sephardic* language is *Ladino* and can be written in Hebrew or Roman characters.

The Ashkenazim greatly outnumber Sephardic Jews. Their various religious, culinary, linguistic and cultural practices vary widely although there are certainly cultural traits and behaviors that are shared by many

Jews. This adds to the comfort they share as descendents of the original families of Israel.

Diasporas

After Israel fell to Assyria in 722 B.C. and Judah fell to Babylon in 597 B.C., the great period of the First Diaspora (dispersion) began. Many Jews moved north to Syria, Cilicia and Caesarea. Others moved east through Persia and south to India and Ceylon. The ten "lost tribes of Israel" which left Babylon following the Assyrian conquests were victims of the Diaspora, or scattering of Israelites. Some are the progenitors of the Anglo-Saxon (Saxon: from "Isaac's sons") tribes, which civilization gave rise to the Celtic peoples and their Druidic priests, as well as to the Teutonic, Irish, Scottish and Welsh races. *(See Drama of the Lost Disciples.)*

By A.D. 300 Jews had settled in every part of the Roman Empire except Britain. They were guaranteed freedom of religion and were allowed other worship rituals. But they found greater freedom under Muslim rule in the decades from A.D. 750 through 1900, although there was continual danger from anti-Jewish discrimination, violence and persecution. During the period between 1000-1500 whole Jewish communities were expelled from western and central Europe, resettling in Italy, Poland and the Ottoman Empire. There they eventually faced further expulsion and mass murder.

Wandering Hebrews have mingled, settled and intermarried with the world's populations through time. There are numerous racial groups worldwide still calling themselves Jews: Caucasian, Black, Arabic, Italian, Chinese, Nordic, and numerous others.

Jews of Spain and Portugal had to face the Inquisition. Those under Turkish rule from 1500 through 1914 found refuge from Spanish and Cossack persecution. Truly, the Jewish people have wandered the earth seeking refuge, peace and prosperity. Until Israel was founded in 1948, they were homeless, although they are still besieged in their Zion.

There is a Christian legend (not in the Gospels), which relates that while Jesus was carrying his cross to Calvary he paused, hoping to rest on a Jew's doorstep. The man at once drove him away crying out "Go hence, go hence!" Jesus then replied "I go, but ye will roam the earth until I come again."

Jewish People In Spiritual Diaspora

Since that time in history the Jewish people have been disunited and scattered. Is there any wonder why? The prophets of old commanded them to hearken and to obey their Law; they did not. They were invited to come unto Christ in the days of the Savior; many would not. They were told that Jesus was the mark they sought, but they stumbled because *they sought beyond the mark.*

Prophecy has come true. In the stead of desecrated and destroyed temples, Jews have no central unifier. They worship in small meetinghouses—synagogues. They look forward dimly to a rebuilt temple in Jerusalem on the site of the Arab-claimed Dome of The Rock, where animal sacrifices will resume. They are engaged constantly in a fight to hold onto their promised land, their Zion, which has instead become a bloody battlefield and prophecy promises near-annihilation in the coming years.

They have no priesthood. They have no ordinances that will save them from this world and they are unaware any are needed. Their heritage is in ruins. Their hope is built upon Israel, which on every side is besieged. They have limited knowledge of Heavenly Father's Plan for them. They are persecuted on every front. The Holocaust of the 1930's and 1940's did much to weaken the faith of many, not to mention the huge destruction of families. Intermarriage has divided their loyalties and caused many to forsake their heritage as Jews. Throughout history hundreds of millions of Jews have died for their beliefs and their cultural ways. Some of these beliefs are founded on correct principles but are misinterpreted and misunderstood in application.

The Jewish people need the tribal family of Ephraim to find them and bring them back to their restored temples and to their glorious destiny.

The Sacred Books of the Jews

Torah (Law)

Torah is the sacred set of teachings from God to the Jews who believe it was given to Moses by God. The Jewish people do not refer to these writings as "Old Testament" writings, because this implies there is a New Testament! The five books of Moses are the essential *Torah*. The "codes" of these writings have three general categories:

- **Commandments**; laws of divine institution and establishment, including the moral law;

- **Ordinances** or the spiritual code; descriptions of the Tabernacle, the Holy Days, the Levitical offerings, daily activity of the priesthood;

- **Judgements**; the social code. Questions of diet, sanitation, quarantine, soil conservation, taxation, military service, how to spend a honeymoon, what to do about divorce, slavery, inheritances, etc.

Until the discovery of the Dead Sea Scrolls the oldest Hebrew manuscripts at our disposal, other than a few fragments, were dated no earlier than the ninth century A.D. Manuscripts of *Torah* books were found in the Judean Desert in 1947. Some of these copies were a thousand years older than those that had been available to biblical scholars up to that point.

The original manuscripts have of course disappeared through the years and wars of the Jews. No extant Hebrew manuscripts date back further than 100 B.C. Because the sacred books were acknowledged as authoritative in Israel, they were consequently set apart from other literature, giving rise to the biblical canon. Concern for a correct text began to grow.

Hebrew words for the five books of *Torah* are:

Genesis	B'resheet
Exodus	Sh'mot
Leviticus	Vayikra
Numbers	B'midbar
Deuteronomy	D'varim *(Mishnah Torah)*

These records of the people who became a Jewish nation describe a fabric, a household: *Bet Yisroel*, the House of Israel. They are a set of traditions and experiences that have molded the Jewish people and have bound them into a family. What we read as the Old Testament discloses central themes that can teach us about essential themes in life, such as service, sin, repentance, faith, longsuffering, love and hate. This testament is a fascinating cornucopia of human experience and an infallible record of how the Lord works in the affairs of men.

These central themes do more than define the Hebrew/Jewish people than all other writings about them. Why is that? Because those who wrote the stories and who faithfully tried to tell of the workings of God and His Chosen people really were the shapers of Judaism itself. These authors, scribes, prophets and priests of hymns, prophecies and laws put down their words in the period between 800-400 B.C. These became the essential compilation of *Torah* in the larger sense. Latter day revelation ascribes authorship of the Pentateuch essentially to Moses and to Joshua who wrote of the patriarch's birth and death. But in the Hebrew Bible, which includes the prophets, the *Talmud* and other writings, many other voices are heard.

How did the Hebrew bible and commentaries come into being? Since the time of Avraham the lore and legends of the Israelites have been recorded. They were told and retold by many oral historians and other peoples over thousands of years. Histories, poems, psalms and messianic myths were created and related in households throughout the area of the Levant. (The Levant includes all countries bordering the sea between Greece and Egypt.)

There have been hundreds of biblical writers and contributors to what is referred to by non-Jews as the Old Testament. They laid down information about their views of religion, their beliefs and practices, their attitudes toward Israelites and non-Israelites, and so on. But it took the Exodus from Egypt and the monarchy of King David to profoundly shape the Israelite imagination. The destruction of Jerusalem in A.D 70 and of the foundation of classical rabbinic Judaism as the Jews were exiled to Babylon resulted in the formation of much of the Hebrew bible or *Torah*. The Hebrew bible contains only the 24 Hebrew books and the Song of Songs but excludes all books written in Greek and the Greek supplements of Esther and Daniel. So these fourteen or so centuries were a time when religious experiences and beliefs of various kinds contributed to the Hebrew scriptures. Scribes wrote these down from oral histories which were addressed to and absorbed by ancient Israel.

These writings became the Palestinian and the Babylonian *Torahs*. They are compendiums of ancient Judaic law; lore and theology produced mainly by rabbis who studied in the ancient tradition and who took the place of priests as teachers of the people. These *Torahs* contain creation myths, text discussing the mysteries of life and death and messianic theories.

The five books of Moses were translated into Greek and codified at Alexandria in 285 B.C. They are called the *Septuagint* (*sept oo ah gint*) because they supposedly contains the work of seventy Jewish scholars.

Ancient translations of those Hebrew scriptures were done in Aramaic. Many of them paraphrase scriptures and supplement with literary allusion in addition to the transcribed texts. The Aramaic version of the Hebrew bible is called the *Targum* and has great value for modern scholars.

Pharisees Tampered with Mosaic Law

The newly transcribed *Torah* writings were finally edited in the fifth and sixth centuries after the death of Jesus Christ by the Pharisees, who are similar to the Orthodox rabbinic Jews of today. Because the Pharisees were in a highly political atmosphere, living in Diaspora in Rome, they edited and rewrote many laws for the Jews of their times. It is reasonable to assume they altered those scriptures dramatically.

Talmud

Jewish oral law contained a tradition of questions and answers and commentary upon *Torah* writings that had been gathered throughout centuries. During the time that Jews were forbidden to live in Israel, this oral law, the *Mishnah*, remained uncodified. This was because rabbis still in the Holy Land were constantly consulted from all over Diaspora on acceptable alternates to worship practices. These replies were called the *Responsa.* In many countries outside Israel, Jews were not permitted to practice their religion outwardly. Rabbi Judah Ha Nasi ordered the *Mishnah* written with its *Responsa.* Other writings were eventually added: the *Gemara* (completion) commentary, and the *Aggadah* – stories, legends, proverbs, parables and anecdotes. The Jerusalem *Talmud* was finished in A.D 400. The Babylonian *Talmud*, codified a century later, is four times the size of the Jerusalem *Talmud* and contains 39 volumes.

No attempt was made to connect any *Talmudic* theories to divine revelation or ancient prophetic utterance because the contributors were considered to be men of God and therefore assumed to be without error. The LDS Doctrine and Covenants contains some sections similar to the *Talmud* in theme, but its author is the Savior himself(!) *(See D&C Sec. 1).* There is neither word unnecessary nor any untruth in the Doctrine and Covenants. Anyone exposed to it will be amazed at the ready answers they find to all of life's questions and problems.

Jewish Mysticism: Kaballah

The prime work on mysticism is the *Kaballah*, which comes from a Hebrew root meaning "to receive." It is thus the "received tradition". Its probable roots are in the few centuries before Christ. *Kaballah* is the study of esoteric aspects of the written *Torah*, the Pentateuch. The early prophets were mystics as well as seers and they had prophetic visions in the apocalyptic tradition. Many rabbis and scholars were known to teach mystical theology and practice in the first centuries of the Common Era. These ideas have become integral in Jewish ritual and folklore. Some bear similarity to spiritual truth. Several schools of Judaic teaching were founded upon these thoughts that were passed down through many generations of Jewish life in Diaspora. Technically, these teachings were called, in Greek, Gnosticism, meaning knowledge. Generally speaking, these mystical theories were a way of explaining the universe to questioning minds of the Diaspora and *prior to* the formulation of Christian theology. When the apostles of Christ were proselytizing, some of these teachings were considered heretical. Church leaders were cautioned strongly to fight their influence upon the congregations. During the time of the Great Apostasy, Gnosticism and Docetism were major confusing influences.

Kaballah holds that the world we see is only part of the whole. Our sight is limited. God is infinite. He has poured His light into each thing that is created so that every person carries the Divine light of truth within him or her. He, God, is not separate from creation for even a moment, so each human being carries the stamp of divinity. Mankind's life task according to *Kaballah* is to become "revealed", not "concealed": to be a clear, radiant image of God. Meditation upon the divine name of God is a necessary part of becoming like Him.

The Latter-day Saint can identify with the above but knows more is required. True Christian doctrine teaches that through revelation we learn we are spirit children of our Heavenly Father.Each person, accordingly, is given the Spirit of Christ. Latter-day Saints are given the additional gift of the Holy Ghost who is the third member of the Godhead. He guides and teaches the "spirit of Christ" that is within each of us. The Holy Ghost, also referred to as the Holy Spirit, is the sole revelator of truth. Mankind's life task is to become like God through the covenants and ordinances of His Church. Qualifications for membership include having faith to repentance, baptism by a member of the restored priesthood of God and the reception of the Gift of the Holy Ghost.

There are numerous themes in *Kaballah* which are stressed in all Christian doctrine. I refer essentially to those that delineate mankind's role as teacher of righteousness and disciple of God in the world. Our life mission is to draw closer to Heavenly Father through worship, praise, meditation and good deeds. Other *Kaballistic* doctrines, while novel and interesting, are not familiar as Christian or specific LDS teachings. These are products of the reasoning of rabbinical scholarship throughout centuries without claim to revelatory experiences. In the time of the teachings of the first apostles, the mystic beliefs of the Jews were an impediment. Paul, in his Epistles, cautions continually against allowing the heretical teachings of non-believers to turn away new Christians from the words of Christ. He was eventually unsuccessful in this endeavor and saw much falling away from the preached Gospel before his death.

Basic Jewish Beliefs

Life

Because life is so valuable, Jews are not permitted to do anything that may hasten death, not even to prevent suffering. However, where death is imminent and certain and the patient is suffering, Jewish law does permit one to cease prolonging life artificially. Of the 613 commandments given in *Torah*, only the prohibitions against murder, idolatry, incest and adultery are so important that they cannot be violated to save a life. Judaism not only permits, but also often *requires* a person to violate the commandments if necessary to save life. Doctors are permitted to answer emergency calls on *Shabbat*, even though this may violate many *Shabbat* prohibitions. According to ancient Jewish law and custom, abortions where necessary to save the life of a mother are mandatory.

Resurrection and Reincarnation

There are some mystical schools of thought that believe resurrection is not a one-time event but is an ongoing process. Some sources indicate that reincarnation is a routine process, whiie others indicate that it only occurs in unusual circumstances, where the soul left unfinished business behind. Belief in reincarnation is also one way to explain the traditional Jewish belief that every Jewish soul in history was present at Sinai and agreed to the covenant with God. Another explanation is that the soul exists before the body, and these unborn souls were present in some form at Sinai. Belief in reincarnation is commonly held by many *Chasidic* sects as well as some other mystically-inclined Jews.

The place of spiritual reward for the righteous is often referred to in Hebrew as *Gan Eden* (GAHN ehy-DEHN) (the Garden of Eden). This is not the same place where Adam and Eve were; it is a place of spiritual perfection. Specific descriptions of it vary widely from one source to another. One source says it is the peace that one feels when one experiences the *Ruach ha-Kodesh* (likened to the Holy Spirit). Only the very righteous go directly to *Gan Eden*. The average person descends to a place of punishment and/or purification. This is generally referred to as **Gehinnom** (geh-hee-NOM) (in Yiddish, *Gehenna*), but sometimes as She'ol or by other names.

Their idea of eternal damnation runs counter to the concept of an all-loving God. *Gehinnom* expiates the sins made on earth, but sinners will find rest every Sabbath. According to one mystical view, every sin we commit creates an angel of destruction (a demon), and after we die we are punished by the very demons that we created. Some views see *Gehinnom* as one of severe punishment, a bit like the Christian hell of fire and brimstone. Other sources merely see it as a time when we can see the actions of our lives objectively. The period of time in *Gehinnom* does not exceed 12 months (*Isa.* 66:23, *Mishnah* 2:10), and then the repentant ascends to take his place on *Olam Ha-Ba*, except for the utterly wicked, who continues to live in constant remorse or who are destroyed.

The *Olam Ha-Ba* (welcome to eternity) or afterlife, is a set of Jewish beliefs about what a person experiences after death. Eligibility is determined by a merit system based on our actions, not by who we are or what religion we profess. After a suitable period of "purification", Jews believe they are eligible for "paradise" based upon their devotion to *Torah* and *mitzvot*. Paradise is a place of spiritual reward for the righteous dead who will be brought back to life and given the opportunity to experience the perfected world that their righteousness helped to create. Judaism teaches that death is not the end of human existence. However, because Judaism is primarily focused on life here and now rather than on the afterlife, there is little dogma about the afterlife, which leaves a great deal of room for personal opinion. Some believe in reincarnation and others think that they simply wait until the coming of the Messiah, when they will be resurrected.

Other beliefs are: the return of the Jewish people from their exile among the nations to their home in Israel; the world will recognize the Jewish God as the only true God and the Jewish religion as the only true religion. There will be no murder, robbery, competition or jealousy. There will be no sin. Sacrifices will continue to be brought into a future temple in Jerusalem, but these will be limited to thanksgiving offerings because there will be no further need for expiatory offerings.

Jesus, Yeshua, Jehovah, Moshiach

Jesus. Jesus is not mentioned in *Torah*. Jews believe his earth life did not qualify for status as their *Moshiach, partly* because his circle of followers was small (except for the converts, who were mostly Hebrews), and he seemed to make little impact among the overwhelming majority of his contemporaries or among the millions in Diaspora. Jews believe he was only one of many martyrs. They expected a warrior-like leader to lead them to peace, to declare himself as their anointed one and to fulfill his mission among them. They reject the Christian belief that Jesus of Nazareth came to earth as the only Begotten Son of God; that his mother Mary conceived as a result of the Holy Spirit coming upon her; or that he was their Savior and the *Jehovah* of Avraham; Isaac and Jacob who gave Moses the Ten Commandments. The Jewish people do not accept that Jesus voluntarily gave up his life in behalf of humanity to pay for its sins or that he overcame death and sin through resurrection. They also do not understand that he came to give full spiritual meaning to the Mosaic Law.

The name "Jesus" is a translation of the Greek name "*Iesous*" (pronounced "[ee-**yay**-sooce"). "*Iesous*" was translated into Latin as "Jesu" ("**yay**-soo") and finally into English as "Jesus." "*Iesous*" is itself a translation of another name. According to Matthew 1:21, the meaning of the name that is translated "Jesus" in English means "he will save his people from their sins."

"Prior to Jesus' birth, an angel told Joseph that his intended wife, Mary, still a virgin, would bear a son who must be named Jesus, because the child was destined to save his people from their sins (Matthew 1:21). If we substitute Yeshua (meaning Salvation, a proper name) in place of Jesus, Matthew 1:21 now has meaning for the English reader." From The Sweetest Name I Know, Peter Colon.

Jehovah, Yeshua. In Hebrew, the name "*Yehoshua*" (translated "Joshua" in English) means "the LORD, OR JEHOVAH. A contraction of "*Yehoshua*" in the Hebrew scriptures is in the form of "*Yeshua*," which means, "he will save" *(see Matthew 1:21)*. We find this name in the book of Chronicles as well as in Ezra and Nehemiah where it usually translates to English as "*Jeshua*" and the concatenated (linking together in a series) form of *Yahoshua*, the "LORD who is Salvation.

Messiah, Moshiach. Jews generally do not recognize the teachings of the prophets that explained who their *Moshiach* really is. *(See Isa. 43:1, 3, 11,15, 44:24, 45:15, 21-23, 53: entire).* This name for God represents the Hebrew conception of the divine nature or character and of the relation of God to His people. It represents the Deity as He is known to His worshipers, and stands for all those attributes which He bears in relation to them and which are revealed to them through His activity on their behalf. Jehovah is the name for the "anointed one". He is the great "I Am" and he is the God of Avraham, Isaac and Jacob.

When Will The *Moshiach* Come?

According to Talmudic thought, before the time of the *Moshiach*, there will be war and suffering *(Ezek 38:16)*. When he arrives on earth, it will be a time of wonder, women will give birth painlessly. Chickens will continuously lay eggs and food appears in abundance. The Jews will return to Israel and the Davidic monarchy will be restored as well as Jewish political independence. Messiah will be victorious and rebuild the Temple. He will establish a government in Israel that will be the center of all world government, both for Jews and Gentiles *(Isaiah 2:2-4; 11:10; 42:1)*. He will restore the priesthood and the Temple and traditional sacrifices will be reinstated. It will be a return to the golden age of the Jewish people, a return to Zion. During this time there will be no eating, drinking, procreation, commerce, jealousy, hate or competition. Only the righteous will have crowns enjoying the radiance of the *Sheckinah* (the presence of God). The messiah will be mortal, a descendent of the House of David. Non-Jews will accept Judaism which teaches that God will personally come to dwell on earth when all people have become righteous. Orthodox Jewish children are taught they must live as though they each have responsibility to bring about the messianic age, that he may come at any time.

Although some scholars believed that God has set aside a specific date for the coming of the *Moshiach*, most authority suggests that the conduct of mankind will determine the time. In general, it is believed that the *Moshiach* will come in a time when he is most needed (because the world is so sinful), or in a time when he is most deserved (because the world is so good). For example, each of the following has been suggested as the time when the *Moshiach* will come:

- If Israel repented a single day.
- If Israel observed a single *Shabbat* properly.
- If Israel observed two *Shabbat*s in a row properly.
- In a generation that is totally innocent or totally guilty.
- In a generation that loses hope.
- In a generation where children are totally disrespectful towards their parents and elders.

BYU Professor Robert Millet tells us: "The law was, as Paul observed, a 'schoolmaster' (literally, pedagogue or supervisor of children) for a wayward people in need of structure and direction. *(Gal. 3:24.)* Unfortunately, the law wasn't sufficient for the Jewish elders. To it, and often replacing it, was added the oral law of the Pharisees. Often called 'the tradition of men' or 'the traditions of the fathers' *(Mark 7:8; Gal. 1:14)*, these interpretations and commentaries on the law in large measure came to govern Jewish life. HAD the Pharisees been more intense in their study of the law itself rather than in the commentaries upon it, they might have recognized Jesus as the promised Messiah. And had they been more eager to apply its teachings rather than to seek for further things they could not understand, they might have been able to accept him. Such, however, was not the case.

"Jesus knew that Judaism carried the promise of salvation, telling a Samaritan woman that 'salvation is of the Jews.' *(John 4:22.)* Yet the failure of individuals to accept living oracles resulted in the Lord's rejection of them. Jesus made this clear when the Pharisees asked why he did not receive them:

'Then said the Pharisees unto him, Why will ye not receive us with our baptism, seeing we keep the whole law?'

'But Jesus said unto them, ye keep not the law. If ye had kept the law, ye would have received me, for I am he who gave the law.

'I receive not you with your baptism, because it profiteth you nothing.''' (JST, Matt. 9:18-20.) *Looking beyond the mark: Why Many Did Not Accept The Messiah. Robert L. Millet, Ensign, July 1987, pg. 60.*

Prophets and Prophecy

A prophet's task is to admonish people from sin and guide them to God. He also warns of coming punishments. No matters of law can be decided by prophecy or any other form of divine inspiration. Today, prophecy is thought by the Jews to be non-existent but will be reinstated with the advent of the *Moshiach*.

Foremost among the gifts of the early Hebrew prophets is the bestowal by God of the Avrahamic covenant upon the seed of Avraham, Isaac and Jacob. Br. Madsen reminds us "the God of Abraham and of Isaac and of Jacob is the living God who led Abraham, the father of nations, out of the throes of idolatry. These Abrahamic traditions are not muted but magnified in Latter-day Saint texts. *(See Pearl of Great Price: Abraham 1:2, 2:8-10 and 3:22-23)". From Chosenness: Implications and Extensions in Mormonism and Judaism , by Truman G. Madsen.*

It would be respectful for LDS to learn and refer to biblical people when talking with Jewish acquaintances. Many Jewish folk respect those who have knowledge of other cultures as well as their own. Here are the Hebrew and the Anglicized names of some significant biblical characters:

Joshua	*Yehoshua*	Nehemiah	*Nechemyahu*
Samuel	*Sh'mu'el*	Matthew	*Mattit'yahu*
Isaiah	*Yesha'yahu*	John	*Yochanan*
Jeremiah	*Yirme'yahu*	James	*Ya'akov*
Ezekiel	*Yechezk'el*	Jude	*Y'hudah*
Joel	*Yo'el*	Peter	*Kefa*
Malachi	*Mal'akhi*		

Redemptive Role of Judah

Prominent men of Christendom have throughout history labeled Jews as inferior to themselves and to humanity. But Latter-day Saints know their indebtedness to the legacy of this people is ordained of God through latter-day scripture and voiced by latter-day prophets. *(See Teachings of the*

Prophet Joseph Smith, by Joseph Fielding Smith). Joseph Smith saw himself as a lineal and spiritual heir of the ancient Joseph and of Ephraim, called to "the role of reconciliation of Judah and Joseph in the last days." *(See Isa 11:13).* He saw the "uniting and reuniting of the entire family of Abraham; and finally of the whole human family."

Other contributions of the Jewish people throughout world history to LDS life are plentiful. Several of those which have directly underscored Christian theology and all true principles are: Jesus the Christ (*Yeshua*, the Messiah), the pre-exilic and many post-exilic prophets of God, revelation, Mosaic Law (including the commandments), the priesthoods, English common law theory and practices derived from the Exodus wanderings. The Israelites were the among the first temple worshippers. They observed sacred ordinances, practiced washing and anointing and other sacred worship practices including Sabbath observances. Many Dead Sea Scroll writings foretold modern prophecy. *Torah* writings are the basis of modern scriptures. The prophets who wrote the Golden Plates which became the Book of Mormon were influenced by ancient Judaic history and writings.

An 1823 revelation received by the Prophet Joseph Smith set into motion events leading to publication of the Book of Mormon. It demonstrated his enduring interest in the Jewish people and a restored Israel. Upon reading the eleventh chapter of Isaiah regarding the coming of a messianic kingdom of righteousness and peace and the gathering of Israel, the core terms and blueprint for the restoration movement was provided the prophet. Thereafter, the reconciliation and gathering between Gentiles and Jews figured prominently in the Book of Mormon and were preoccupations of Smith. *(Adapted from Mormons and Jews. Early Mormon Theologies of Israel, by Steven Epperson, p.21).*

Learning Through Symbols

"His (Jesus') blood has atoned, once and for all, for all of mankind's sin, beginning with Adam and Eve. The symbol of the fire has been replaced by the cleansing power of the Holy Ghost through symbolic anointing of the offerer with olive oil *(D&C 45:55-57).* The oil suggests that the Spirit's effect upon those organs, which had been cleansed by the blood of Christ, is to purify and sanctify the individual so that he can come into the proper relationship with God." *(From Old Testament Types and Symbols, by Gerald Lund, in Literature of Belief, pp. 40-59).*

Each event is symbolic, but in order to interpret them correctly, several steps must be taken. Dr. Lund lists them as follows:

- *Look beyond the symbol for its intended meaning*

- *Look for the interpretation of the symbol in the scriptures themselves*
- *Look for Christ in the symbols and imagery of the scriptures*
- *Let the nature of the object used as a symbol contribute to your understanding of its spiritual meaning*
- *Seek the reality behind the symbol*

To add to Dr. Lund's advice, look also at the arrangement and meaning of Hebrew letters and words. Each Hebrew letter has both a temporal and spiritual meaning. All Hebrew letters have multiple meanings. When arranged in words these letters can be read as stand-ins for objects, ideas or themes that convey messages. This in itself is a scholarly study that can occupy a lifetime while bringing great fruit of understanding.

For example, reading from right to left:

The Hebrew word for truth or faithfulness is *emeth* (אֱמֶת). The first letter is an *aleph,* which can mean "primal energy". The second letter is a *mem* and can mean "water flow or purification". The final letter is a *tav* which can mean "*path to perfection*". Truth, as the Jewish scholar interprets it is the beginning, middle and end of all things. Mormons interpret truth according to the guidelines stated in D&C 93:24-25, below.

And truth is knowledge of things as they are, and as they were, and as they are to come; and whatsoever is more or less than this is the spirit of that wicked one who was a lier from the beginning.

Another example is the Hebrew word for remember: *zachor* (זכור). The first letter is *zayin,* which can mean a sharp tool, drawing blood. The second letter is *kaf.* Its usual representation is a bent or cupped hand. The *vav* (third letter) can mean a nail, whereas the final letter, *resh,* means head. The interpretation that would be made here is that the sharp tool, the nail, drew blood from the hand of the man whose identity was at his head on the cross, i.e. "King Of The Jews". He allowed himself to die for our transgressions. It should be obvious that a Jewish reader would have other interpretations.

Other Jewish rituals also bear the sacrifice-atonement-life symbology that defines the essence of Christianity. They are too numerous to name here. Several especially significant examples are: the Hebrew ordinance of circumcision, the Sabbath observance, the Seven Feasts of Israel (described in this book), Avraham's willingness to sacrifice his son, Isaac, and the Exodus of the Israelites from Egypt.

Dr. Lund points out that the reality behind the Old Testament is Jesus Christ and his doctrine of salvation. The better we understand it, the more clearly we will see the meaning of the symbols. This is what the Jews did not learn, and what they must learn in the coming events which are spelled out in prophetic utterances throughout messianic scripture.

Worship and Religious Practices

Shabbat (Sabbath)

What does the Exodus have to do with resting on the seventh day? It's all about freedom. By resting on *Shabbat*, people are reminded that they are free. *Shabbat* frees from our weekday concerns, much as the Hebrews were freed from slavery in Egypt. Jews recite *kiddush* (the prayer over wine) sanctifying *Shabbat* on Friday at sundown as a memorial of the work in the beginning of time and a remembrance of the Exodus.

According to *Torah*, no one should do physical labor, buy or sell or expend effort on *Shabbat*. Rabbis cannot lead the service, nor can creative endeavor be undertaken. In the lives of observant Jews, two *Shabbat* candles are lit and a blessing is recited no later than eighteen minutes before sunset. This ritual, performed by the woman of the house, officially marks the beginning of *Shabbat*. The candles represent the two commandments: *zachor* (remember) and *shamor* (observe). The family then attends a brief evening service followed by dinner. Before dinner, a *Bar-Mitzvahed* Jewish male of the house recites *Kiddush*, a prayer over wine sanctifying *Shabbat*. The usual prayer for eating bread is recited over two loaves of *challah*, a sweet, eggy bread shaped in a braid. After dinner, the *birkat ha-mazon* (grace after meals) is recited.

The next morning *Shabbat* services begin around 9 am and continue until about noon. After services, the family says *kiddush* again and has another leisurely, festive meal. *Shabbat* ends at nightfall, when three stars are visible, approximately 40 minutes after sunset. At the conclusion of *Shabbat* the family performs a concluding ritual called *Havdalah* (separation, division). Blessings are recited over wine, spices and candles. Then a blessing is recited regarding the division between the sacred and the secular, between *Shabbat* and the working day, and so on.

Priesthood

Aaronic. The *kohanim* (Aaronic priesthood holders in ancient times), and Levites are the direct descendants of Aaron, chosen by God at the time of the incident with the Golden Calf *(Ex 32:8-28)* to perform certain sacred work, particularly in connection with animal sacrifices and the rituals related to the Temple. The fundamental ideas that underlie this office were reconciliation and mediation; the one expressed by atoning sacrifices, the other by intervening priesthood. After the destruction of the Temple, the role of the *kohanim* diminished significantly in favor of the rabbi*s*.

A study published in *Nature* in June 1997 shows that self-identified *kohanim* in three countries have common elements in the Y-chromosome, indicating that *they all have a common male ancestor*. This DNA research supports the fact that the tribes of Israel are indeed racially descended.

Today's Jews do not hold any priesthood or claim to know in large part their line of patriarchal descendency. Some believe they are descended from Judah, Aaron or Levi.

When the Temple of Herod was destroyed in A.D. 70, all priesthood observances ceased.

Melchizedek. Probably from Malachi, meaning "my messenger" (pronounced mel **chi** zedek) (righteousness, justice, equity/fairness). Refers to the holy order of God or higher priesthood. The Prophet Joseph Smith taught:

"All the prophets had the Melchizedek Priesthood and were ordained by God himself." Further: "Was the Priesthood of Melchizedek taken away when Moses died? All priesthood is Melchizedek, but there are different portions or degrees of it. That portion which brought Moses to speak with God face to face was taken away; but that which brought the ministry of angels remained". *From Teachings of the Prophet Joseph Smith, pp 180-81.*

This higher priesthood is not familiar to modern Jewry, nor has the author ever come across the word with reference to ancient tabernacles or early temple duties of Hebrew high priests. Though, all true prophets as well as the priests who entered the Holy of Holies area of Israelite tabernacles and early temples most certainly held the Melchizedek priesthood.

Tabernacles, Temples

To the Hebrews, the First and Second Temples were akin to palaces dedicated to God. The primitive Tabernacle in the desert was the first Israelite temple *(Ex 24, 25, Lev 9,10)*. Its dimensions doubled were the architectural base for the Temple of Solomon. The first temple was dedicated by Solomon in Jerusalem in 950 B.C. but destroyed in 587 B.C. by Nebuchadnezzar. Zerubab**bel** (seed of Babel) rebuilt it in 516 B.C. (Ezra 3.3) but it lacked the Ark of the Covenant, the *Sheckinah*, the *Urim* and *Thummim (Ezra 2:63)*, the holy altar fire and the spirit of prophecy. (LDS Bible Dictionary, p. 783). King Herod added to that about 20 B.C. The Roman army destroyed the edifice in A.D. 70 and burned Jerusalem. Israel has designated the ancient site for a new temple but has not as yet begun building, as the holy site is adjacent the Dome of the Rock on the Temple Mount.

There were deep meanings associated with the physical dimensions and plans for the tabernacle. They were meant to reflect spiritual patterns that are also reflected in the temples of today. The Ark of the Covenant, the repository of the commandments that were given to Moses was in Solomon's temple but had disappeared by the time Herod's temple was built.

Because the small ark was portable and carried from place to place, and because the tabernacle was also mobile, the Hebrew people imagined that their Deity lived in the Ark and in the incense the priests waved around and therefore added to their belief that God is not containable in a body.

Only the chosen high priest could enter the Holy of Holies room, equivalent to the celestial room in restored LDS temples. Typically, he had a rope tied to an ankle so that if he died while in that room with his Maker, he could be pulled out; no one else was permitted to enter and retrieve him.

People have always needed temples. In the ancient world of the Jews Josephus tells us the first temple was built on Mt. Gerizim, with Manasseh as its first high priest. The 13th chapter of Nehemiah probably refers to this event. The LDS Bible Dictionary tells us that it became the refuge of all Jews who had violated the precepts of the Mosaic Law. That temple was destroyed in 109 B.C.

Solomon's temple was next, as we are told in 1Kings and 2 Chronicles. It was consecrated in the 10th century during a Feast of Tabernacles and the Feast of Dedication lasted 14 days. We read in 2 Kings 25 that it was burned to the ground by Nebuchadnezzar (really Nebuchadrezzar. It had stood 410 years. The holy Ark of the Covenant was probably stolen from it, and no one knows today where it is.

The temple of Zerubba**bel** was erected to be essentially a reproduction of Solomon's, dedicated in 516 B.C., recorded in Ezra 6. It, too, was desolated and burned, only to have of Herod Herod rebuild it, but that beautiful structure also knew destruction when in A.D. 70 Jerusalem was burned. It had stood 420 years. In architectural splendor, this edifice outshined Solomon's temple but the real elements of temple glory had disappeared. The Holy of Holies was empty, the ark with the tables of the law, the book of the covenant, Aaron's rod that budded and the pot of manna were no longer in the sanctuary. The fire that had descended from heaven was now extinct. And the visible presence of God in the *Sheckinah* was wanting. The will of God could not be discerned from the *Urim* and *Thummim*, nor could the high priest be anointed with holy oil, because no one could be sure it was pure. And then there were the Pharisees, who specialized in aborting and reworking the pure Mosaic Law given to their prophet, Moses, by the holy One of Israel.

Kosher Laws

The laws of *kashrut* allow enjoyment of the pleasures of the physical world, sanctifying and elevating the pleasure through consciousness and sensitivity. *Kashrut* recognizes that the essential human need is not food, drink or comfort, but meaning. Judaism, through the dietary laws, injects meaning even into something as commonplace and instinctive as eating. Judaism seeks to elevate the physical world, not to deny it, nor to glorify it.

Many animals are unclean and have unclean diets. In an effort to keep the Israelites somewhat assimilated and separated from the pagan societies they lived in as captives, these rules helped to insure the people would have healthy and safe dietary habits.

It is forbidden to cook, eat, or benefit from milk and meat mixtures but there are some foods which are considered neutral and these can be mixed with meat or dairy. It is also forbidden to cook or eat dairy products together with poultry. Milk products (including the rennet in cheese) must only come from kosher animals. *(See Leviticus 11 and Deuteronomy 14).*

A kosher animal must be a ruminant (chew their cuds) and have split hooves. Most common fowl are kosher, but birds of prey are not kosher because they hunt and eat unclean flesh. A sea creature is only kosher if it has fins and scales. Shellfish are not kosher; dolphins, whales and squids are also not kosher. Any food product of a non-kosher animal is also non-kosher, such as their eggs or milk. The exception to this rule is bee's honey.

An animal or bird must be slaughtered according to Jewish law (*shechita*). This involves cutting the animal's trachea and esophagus (the carotid and jugular are also severed) with a surgically sharp knife. The cut must be swift, continuous and performed by an expert. The animal must not suffer if possible. This method of slaughter reduces the blood pressure in the brain to zero immediately, so that the animal loses consciousness in a few seconds and dies in minutes.

The animal or bird must be free of injuries, diseases or abnormalities whose presence renders the animal non-kosher. It is possible that one idea behind this is to encourage us to view ourselves with dignity and to act with dignity. One of the best defenses against immorality is a strong sense of self-esteem and dignity.

Certain fats may not be eaten. Blood must be removed from the meat, either by soaking, salting and rinsing or by broiling. The sciatic nerve in each leg and the surrounding fat must be removed.

Shofar

The *shofar* is a ram's horn, symbolizing the animal that appeared as a substitute for Isaac when his father Abraham was ready to sacrifice him upon at altar. Used on official occasions, and in Israel at start of *Shabbat*. There is order to the nature, sequence and frequency of the blasts blown from the smaller end of the horn, which is not supposed to be altered in any way. Rabbis developed elaborate rules that state broken notes should resemble sobbing, that a long unbroken note must precede and follow the broken ones. Many Jews speculate the Advent of their *Moshiach* will be heralded by the sound of a *shofar* and that God will use the *shofar* to deliver the trump sound of the Advent of the *Moshiach*.

Washings

Currently both male and female converts to Judaism are immersed (tavilah) in the *mikvah* (a ritual bath used for spiritual purification), as part of the process of spiritual cleanliness. This does not have exactly the same significance as it does for Christians. Note that there was a Jewish custom of washing the priest's feet that may relate to Jesus washing feet of a disciple described in the New Testament. This was not to be confused with a religious ritual, and may have been more of a social custom.

Jewish Congregations: Detail

Orthodox

Orthodox and sometimes Conservative congregations are described as "traditional" movements. Orthodox Judaism observances hail back to past centuries, eschewing progressive movements. Reverence is always shown for the customs of the past, no changes are permitted. Examples: A woman's place is only in the home. Kosher dietary laws are followed. Scriptures are read in Hebrew. Circumcision is practiced on every Jewish male at eight days of life. Strict interpretation of *Torah* is mandatory. The rabbi is revered; he is usually a man with academic training, but is always a scholar of Judaism. In Orthodox and Chasidic practice, women are not permitted to participate in religious services in these ways. The boys and girls in an Orthodox congregation are expected to be *Bar* or *Bat Mitzvah*ed. The *Torah* and Talmudic laws are considered the final authority in all cases. *Yarmulkes* (skullcaps worn by male Jews) or other hats men wear show their obedience to God and set them apart as a special group.

Rules concerning the Sabbath are very strict and all encompassing, from writing and using the telephone to taking a prescribed number of steps between home and synagogue. Orthodoxy subscribes to the 13 principles of Faith codified by the Sephardic rabbi Moshe Ben Maimonides (see page 77). Orthodox Jews believe they were exiled from their homeland because of disobedience to *Torah* laws and that when all of Jewry truly repents and lives in accordance with the commandments, the exile will be ended, the Jews will return to their homeland *en masse* and the Temple will be rebuilt there. Often, Jews refer to their synagogue as a temple, but this is incorrect usage relative to the ordinances performed in ancient Israelite temples and LDS temples.

Conservative

This is a liberal or modern movement. It is slowly evolving as it synthesizes with American life. Scriptures are read in Hebrew and English. Updated versions of the *Siddur* or songbook are used.

Conservative Judaism grew out of the tension between Orthodoxy and Reform congregations. Conservatives generally accepts the binding nature of *halakhah*, or the Jewish way, but believes the Law should change and adapt. There is a great deal of variation among Conservatives. Most are very traditional in substance, if not always in form. Originally it was an attempt to Americanize the millions of migrating Eastern European Jews during early part of 20th century. This congregational approach has evolved. We find organs in synagogues. Men and women sit together through the services. Increasingly, women are being called to stand in *minyan*s as well as to read *Torah*. In 1985, women were allowed to be ordained rabbis. Some rules prohibiting communication and travel have been liberalized. Skullcaps are not required outside of worship services or when reading sacred texts. Dietary laws are relaxed, also. Conservative rabbis cannot officiate at the marriage of a Jew to a non-Jew, but Reform rabbis may do so.

Reform

These congregations are also "liberal" or "modern" movements, moving with the mainstream of American life. Many things differ from Orthodox worship practices. One is not required to cover one's head during worship. Prayer and readings are in English. *Torah* is binding only ethically, it is not read as a divine instruction manual. Diversity of life is promoted. Reform congregations do not believe that *Torah* was written by God but by separate sources and redacted together. Reform Jews do not believe in observance of commandments as such, but they retain much of the values and ethics of Judaism, along with some of the practices and the culture. Many non-observant, nominal, and/or agnostic Jews identify themselves as Reform simply because Reform is the most liberal movement which adopts a modern, rationalistic approach to *halakhah*. Prayers have been shortened and may be said in the vernacular of the country instead of Hebrew. Reform Jews wait for a "messianic age", rather than a Messiah. They use mixed choirs in services. Dietary restrictions and the need for ritual dress has been eliminated.

Reconstructionist

Founded by Mordechai Kaplan, this has recently become one of the major divisions of American Jewry. Kaplan emphasized the people-hood of all Jews regardless of theological beliefs and an organized Jewish community life. Jewish law and custom is regarded as a "folkway" that should be preserved as much as possible as expressions of the Jews. God, to Kaplan, is a "Power in the universe sympathetic to humanity." God is also a "Process" useful for making righteousness and a meaningful life. This movement operates within the three other major groups. Advocates may be radical feminists or vegetarians, and may use the term "new age" in their belief system. *(From The Concise Guide to Judaism; History, Practice, Faith, by Rabbi Roy A. Rosenberg.)*

Messianism

The Messianics are not a Jewish movement, but boasts congregants who believe Jesus (*Yeshua*) is the Redeemer spoken of in the *Tanakh* and that he is the world's Messiah. Jews for Jesus is one group. These congregations are a recent phenomenon and growing rapidly. They refer to their places of worship as synagogues and worship on the traditional Jewish Sabbath (Friday sundown/Saturday sundown). They uphold some basic Mosaic Law practices but live a New Covenant lifestyle. Members believe they are saved by faith. They reject the Christian Jesus in favor of the "Jewish *Yeshua*" because they don't identify with the Greek Gentile concept of Jesus. They try to reflect the Jewishness of their faith to Jews. Their services are quite different from any other congregation. A Messianic rabbi conducts. Many members are not even Jewish! Worship involves much singing and dancing. They have been greatly influenced by *Chasidism*, meaning "pious ones". Messianic Jews don't accept the *Talmud* as word of God. They believe spiritual progression through enlightenment does not come from *Torah*, and they believe the world is moving toward a time of true peace. This group might be most easily brought to the true Gospel.

Chasidim or Hasidism

This is a vital movement in Orthodox Jewry throughout the world; its influences are felt within Messianic, Samaritan, and other groups. This, the first of the modern movements, was developed in Eastern Europe in the 1700's by Rabbi Israel Baal Shem Tov (Master of the Good Name). Before *Chasidism*, Judaism emphasized education as the way to get closer to God, emphasizing other, more personal experiences including mysticism as alternative routes to God. So many of the Polish poor and sick Jews needed a way to surmount their plight, so the Baal Shem Tov taught that God pays heed to worship only when it is offered in joy. Song and dance should accompany prayer, for true piety exists only when one is exhilarated by the sense of God's presence.

Chasidic sects are organized around a spiritual leader called a *rebbe* or a *tzaddik*, a person who is considered to be more enlightened than other Jews. A *Chasid* consults his *rebbe* about all major life decisions. *Chasids* believe the way to worship God is through joyous acclamation, dancing, singing and loudly praising. They use parables and stories to promote encouragement and inspiration. God, they believe, needs mankind's redemptive acts, so every Jew has a role to fulfill. If every task is performed as a *mitzvah* (commandment) to God, then it will be a response to the Father.

Leadership in Synagogue

Gabbai A *gabbai* is a layperson who volunteers to perform various duties in connection with *Torah* readings at religious services. Serving as a *gabbai* is a great honor, and is bestowed on a person who is thoroughly versed in *Torah* and *Torah* readings.

Tzaddik *Tzaddik* literally means "righteous one." It also generally indicates that the person has spiritual or mystical power. A *tzaddik* is not necessarily a rabbi, but *Chasidic* rabbis are *tzaddiks*.

Major Jewish Holidays

Festival of Esther (Purim)	Mar 14
Passover (Pesach)	Apr 13-20
33rd Day of Omer (Lag B'Omer)	May 16
Feast of Weeks (Shavuot)	Jun 2-3
Feast of Trumpets (Rosh Hashonah)	Oct 3-4
Day of Atonement (Yom Kippur)	Oct 13
Feast of Tabernacles (Sukkot)	Oct 18-24
Festival of Lights (Chanukah)	Dec 26-Jan2

Purim - Book of Esther

The story of *Purim* is told in the book of Esther. *Purim* is celebrated on the 14th day of Ad*ar*, which is usually in March. The 13th of *Adar* is the day that Haman chose for the extermination of the Jews, and the day that the Jews battled their enemies for their lives. On the day afterwards, the 14th, they celebrated their survival. In cities that were walled in the time of Joshua, *Purim* is celebrated on the 15th of the month.

The book of Esther is unusual in that it is the only book of the Bible that does not contain the name of God. In fact, it includes virtually no reference to God. Mordecai makes a vague reference to the fact that the Jews will be saved by someone else, if not by Esther, but that is the closest the book comes to mentioning God. Thus, one of the important messages that can be gained from the story is that God often works in ways that are not apparent, in ways that to us appear to be chance, coincidence or ordinary good luck.

Perhaps the most significant fact to Christianity of the Purim holiday is that it is celebrated on the 14th of Adar in the ancient Jewish lunar calendar. This date translates to April 6 in our Gregorian calendar. Many believe the 14th of Adar was the birth date of Jesus. According to some scholars, it was also on this day in A.D. 37(or 34), during the 23-year reign of Emperor Tiberius (A.D. 14-37), that the Savior of the world was crucified. The Church of Jesus Christ of Latter-day Saints was officially organized April 6, 1830. It is also believed by many that the Exodus of the Israelites from Egypt began on that day.

Passover/Feast of the Unleavened Bread

During the *seder* (order) meal, ritual questions are asked about the past and present. Jews celebrate the Feast of Unleavened Bread at the

Passover, which we compare to the death and resurrection of Christ. During the Passover meal a broken piece of *matzoh* (unleavened bread) is put into a white bag and hidden nearby. This is called the *afikomen (hidden),* that which is eaten afterward, the dessert. The *seder* cannot end without the return of this piece of unleavened bread. After the meal it is "found" again. Jews relate that to the ancient paschal lamb. They don't understand it is an act in similitude of the body of Christ buried and resurrected *(See Matt 26:26).* Unleavened bread is baked for exactly 18 minutes, 18 meaning chai, or life—making it the bread of life.

The leaven in bread is an agent of change that invites distortion from truth, it destroys the purity of the seed. The covering of the hidden bread symbolizes to us the tomb from which Jesus arose and as the tomb becomes empty, Christ, the living seed of the living God, rises from the tomb, so the bread is brought forth.

The seed itself buried in earth rises from its tomb as wheat without leaven, becoming bread. The seed is known by its fruit, it is free of the stains of the world. The word Bethlehem *(Bet lechem)* in Hebrew means house of bread. From the coffin (seed), comes the fruit (the spirit that rises to everlasting life).

To honor the future, a glass of wine is set aside for Elijah, who will come to tell of the arrival of the *Mashiach* and rescue the Jews from oppression. (They are still waiting.) It is noteworthy that the holiday is called the time of the *giving* of *Torah*, rather than the time of the *receiving* of *Torah*. The sages point out that we are constantly in the process of receiving *Torah*, that we receive it every day, but it was first given at this time. Thus it is the giving, not the receiving that makes this holiday significant.

Egypt can be seen as reminiscent of Babylon or the wicked world. Israel was slave to the Egyptians, as we in our sins are in bondage to the Adversary. Following nine of the ten plagues the Lord visited upon the Egyptians, their first-born sons were slain. The Israelites were commanded to put lamb's blood on the lintel and two side posts of their homes with the herb hyssop, symbol of purification. Destroying angels passed them by. *Their* firstborn sons were saved by the "blood of the lamb" *(1 Ne 12:10, D&C 76:69)* that was to be *Yeshua*, the deliverer, their salvation, Jesus, who would die to atone for the sins of the world and rise again to eternal life.

After Pharaoh's first-born son was slain, he freed the Israelite slaves. This was a symbol of the liberating mission to mankind, which *Yeshua* (Jesus) promises, as well as the promise of life through the Firstborn of the Father.

The Israelites were commanded to roast a lamb with its entrails intact, letting out the blood only. As the Son gave himself entirely upon the cross, so the *paschal* lamb was entirely consumed without a bone broken. See Psalms 34:20 and Jn 19:36 for prophecy fulfilled that not a bone of His would be broken when he was crucified. The atonement of Jesus Christ must be partaken of and entirely absorbed to give us spiritual strength and sustenance.

The Exodus followed. In its desert wanderings the new Hebrew nation ate manna that was called "bread from heaven" *(Ex. 16:4)*. In like manner, Jesus has said he is the living bread, which came down from heaven.

The Feast of First Fruits, Shavuot

Lev 23:10-14
- Gift of the Holy Ghost the resurrection of the seed.
- Festival for land fertility
- Harvest of wheat, barley
- Resurrection of Christ, the First Fruits

The Feast of *Shavuot* is known in the New Testament as Pentecost, a day where there was a great manifestation of the Holy Ghost and 3,000 Hebrew souls rose from the dead. Jews begin a seven week set of rituals represented by harvesting wheat and barley. The Pentecost is a symbol of the gift of Holy Ghost in which the remnant is fed. *(See Acts 2)*.

Anciently, doves were used as a sin offering. Jesus Christ, then, is as a kernel of wheat in the fire. As the loaves represent sinful men because they contain leaven, Christ is as unleavened bread, the pure, eternal seed that gives life to all creation and from which creation he receives ever more glory. *Shavuot* is remembered as a day of law and lawlessness, when 3,000 were slain because they built idols. On this day also the Hebrew people received from Moses the Ten Commandments. It is celebrated as a time of charity. In Israel, fields are harvested but not the corners of the fields. Those without means, the remnant of society, are permitted to eat their fill. Symbolically, we are the farmers and we are the remnant who are saved and encouraged to feast upon the fruit of the gospel.

Leviticus 23:10 contains the commandment to make a yearly celebration for six of the seven feasts of Israe!. It is a festival for fertility of the land when crops are resurrected and the ground made new. It was a memorable time because of the earthquakes and resurrection of the many dead. *(Matt 27:53-54)*. In this celebration the time is for resurrection of believers, crops, the spring crop of barley that the priest used to wave over his head *(Psalms 1)*. Latter-day Saints know that Jesus is the First Fruits of they who slept and died and we faithful Saints are the second.

Following the Restoration of the Gospel, on *Shavuot*, the second day of Passover April 3, 1836, the Lord appeared in vision to the Prophet Joseph Smith and Oliver Cowdery in the Kirtland Temple. Moses, Elias and Elijah also appeared. They committed to Joseph and Oliver the keys of the gathering of Israel from the four parts of the earth, the leading of the ten tribal families from the north, the administering of the keys of the Avrahamic dispensation, and the keys of sealing powers. *(D&C 110:3-4,7).*

When our Savior rose from the grave he also raised many dead. He made an offering to Heavenly Father on that feast day. He had an appointment to keep: He died in only 6 hours, was buried on Feast of Unleavened Bread day and rose from his grave the next, the First Fruits of they who will live forever. The 3,000 saved Jewish souls who rose with him were an offering to Heavenly Father.

Feast of Trumpets - Rosh Hashonah

Lev 23:24-25
Jewish New Year - Prayers for Israel (Second Coming of Christ)

Prophecy of the return of Christ, the deliverance of mortals from bondage of the Adversary. In Hebrew, *Rosh Hashonah* means "head of the cycle" or "first of the year." The Jewish New Year is a time to begin introspection, looking back at the mistakes of the past year and planning the changes to make in the new year. It commemorates the birthday of the world.

Rosh Hashonah looks toward fulfillment of peace and adjudication of all problems on earth. The **Hosanna** ("save") **Shout** originated here. In this festival Jews celebrate their liberty from Egypt and slavery. It is a feast of deliverance. God will use the ram's horn (*Shofar*) to deliver the trump sound of the Advent of the Savior. *Rosh Hashonah* begins the Ten Days of Penitence (Days of Awe) which end in Yom Kippur services. The traditional greeting is *lashana tova tikusevu*, which means "may you be inscribed for a good year".

Orthodox and Conservative Jews celebrate two days of *Rosh Hashonah*. Reform Jews celebrate only the first.

LDS Connection to Rosh Hashonah

One result of the Prophet Joseph Smith receiving the Golden Plates on *Rosh Hashonah* (see p. 37) was that the heavenly vision of the forces of good vs evil was shown to John P Greene, Brigham Young, John Young, Heber C Kimball--all neighbors-- in Mendon, NY, a short distance north of Palmyra. In June 1830 Samuel Smith, the prophet's brother and the first Mormon missionary, left the first copy of the newly printed Book of Mormon with Rev John P Greene who loaned it to the Youngs and Kimballs. The rest is "history". A new Cycle of God had commenced.

Yom Kippur, Day of Atonement

Lev 23:27-32
- Yearly day of Jewish repentance. A male goat represents sins of people.
- Atonement of Israel at Second Coming of Christ (Christ's shedding of blood for Israel's sins)

The name *Yom Kippur* means "Day of Atonement." It is a day set aside to "afflict the soul," to atone for the sins of the past year. As noted in Days of Awe, *Yom Kippur* atones only for sins between man and God, not for sins against another person. To atone for those sins, first seek reconciliation with that person, righting the wrongs committed against them if possible. That must all be completed before *Yom Kippur*.

Yom Kippur is really a holiday kept in similitude of Christ's atonement, whereas in the days of the temple two goats were chosen by lot. One was designated as the scapegoat, or the goat of Azazel. The second was the goat of the LORD and became a sin offering. Its blood, when applied by the priest to the horns of the scapegoat, symbolically transferred all of the sins of the people of Israel to it. After elaborate prayer by the priest, the scapegoat was sent into the wilderness.

The **Shema** is said and the **shofar** (ram's horn) is blown just before sunset to signify the end of the sacred event. It is blown on three occasions.

1. The first sound from the horn is a call to repentance. The dead are symbolically called to life.

2. The second sound is to remind God that He is in a covenantal relationship with the Jews.

3. The third trump is a call to arms and to confuse Satan the Accuser on the birth of a new year.

The ram's horn also symbolizes the story of Avraham and his willingness to sacrifice his son, Isaac.

Yom Kippur is celebrated only one day everywhere. Paul used the typology of *Yom Kippur* to teach the mission of Christ, who, holy and without spot was the true High Priest, unlike the officiating Israelite priests. *(Heb 3:1 and 7:26-27).* He did not need to atone for sins before he was worthy to officiate for Israel and enter the Holy of Holies as the high priests had to do.

The Feast of Tabernacles - Sukkot

Lev 23:39-43
- 7th full moon of year, symbol of wilderness in Egypt at Exodus
- Coming of Prince of Peace as sanctuary in wilderness

The Festival of *Sukkot* lasts 7 days. The word "*Sukkot*" means "booths" and refers to the temporary dwellings that Jews are commanded to live in during this holiday. The name of the holiday is frequently translated "The Feast of Tabernacles". The process goes from one of the most solemn holidays in our year to one of the most joyous. Like Passover and *Shavuot*, *Sukkot* has a dual significance: historical and agricultural. The holiday commemorates the forty-year period during which the children of Israel were wandering in the desert living in temporary shelters. *Sukkot* is also a harvest festival, the Festival of Ingathering. Along with Passover, it is one of the holy (and happy) times that the Children of Israel were given to remind them of being delivered from bondage.

Sukkot with its lights is also the time to remember Solomon's dedication of the Temple, the Lord's house. The Temple became the symbol that set the people apart from others. They and their Temple were to be an "ensign" to the nations. That ensign was a "light" to the world in its day and would be so again in latter-days.

A feature of Sukkot is that Israel was required to live in homemade tabernacles, not in their homes, reminding them they had lived that way after the Exodus. Elder Bruce R. McConkie stated,

"In its full sense, it is the Feast of Jehovah, the one Mosaic celebration which, as part of the restitution of all things, shall be restored when Jehovah comes to reign personally upon the earth for a thousand years. ... we perform one of its chief rituals in our solemn assemblies, the giving of the Hosanna Shout... The fact that it celebrated the completion of the full harvest symbolizes the gospel reality that it is the mission of the house of Israel to gather all nations to Jehovah..." *The Promised Messiah, Bruce R. McConkie, p.432*

Feast of Lights, Temple Rededication - Chanukah
- Rededication after victory over Alexander's army
- Prophecy of God's temples again on the earth, baptism, endowments

An evil Greek ruler began to oppress the Jews severely, placing a Hellenistic priest in the First Temple, massacring Jews, prohibiting the practice of the Jewish religion, and desecrating the Temple by requiring the sacrifice of pigs (non-kosher animals) on the altar. Two groups opposed him. They joined forces in a revolt. The revolution succeeded and the Temple was rededicated.

According to tradition as recorded in the *Talmud*, at the time of the rededication, there was very little olive oil left that had not been defiled by the Greeks. Oil was needed for the *menorah* (candelabrum) in the Temple, which was supposed to burn throughout the night every night. There was only enough oil to burn for one day, yet miraculously it burned for eight days—the time needed to prepare a fresh supply of oil for the menorah. An eight-day festival was declared to commemorate this miracle. Note that the holiday commemorates the miracle of the oil, not the military victory.

On the first night, only the *shammus* (servant, and a light to all mankind) is lit and one *Chanukah* candle. On each succeeding night one more candle is added to the *menorah*. By the eighth night, all of the eight candles are in place and lit at the start of services with the *shammus*.

Fulfilling the Law and Prophecies

Jesus has completed the first four feasts symbolically by being born, dying and being raised again and restoring the Gospel or Good News. He has yet to come to the Jews (Feast of Trumpets-*Rosh Hashonah*), they must atone for their stubborn refusal to accept him (*Yom Kippur*), and he will instruct them on rebuilding and coming to their temples (Feast of Tabernacles-*Sukkot*). *Chanukah* is really the 8th feast because Passover and the Feast of Unleavened Bread are considered as two feasts in one.

All Righteous Things Testify of Christ

Beyond the Hebrew understanding of the Feasts of Israel and the Christian interpretations of the symbols, there is another way to understand how the Gospel transcends all we do and experience on this earth. For instance, why are there 7 to 9 months of pregnancy?

The exact span of days between *Purim* and *Chanukah* = 280 days or 9 months. (Refer to the calendar of Jewish holy days on page 60.)

Purim Spring fertilizing, conception

Passover, Unleavened Bread Seed buried

Pentecost Seed implantation, first fruits. Becomes fetus in 50 days

Feast of Trumpets Fetus gets hearing ability, 1st day of 7th month

Day of Atonement Fetus' blood matures, 10th day, seventh month

Feast of Tabernacles Lungs mature, 15th day, seventh month

Feast of Lights, rebirth of temple Fetus essentially ready for birth as mortal. Needed strength, size, gained during final two months

Part 3: References

This section provides references for your detailed study. As you see below, it includes an extract from the Orson Hyde prayer, an address by President Benson, and Jewish jokes and recipes. Some of the topics in this section are:

Language references: Hebrew and Yiddish terms, Hebrew is writing pattern, Chiastic structures, and Hebrew "Alefbet".

Law: Maimonides 13 Principles of Faith, and the Seven Laws of Noah.

History: tribes of Israel, significant Judaic scholars, History and events, major changes, modern events, and holocaust. Apostasy.

LDS Perspectives: Orson Hyde Prayer, Ezra Taft Benson message, LDS scriptural Citations.

Cultural and religious practices: Washings, care for the dead and mourning practices, Hebrew calendar, and Jewish recipes and jokes.

For basic understanding (less detailed study), please start with Part 1. For detailed study, see Part 2.

Language

Glossary of Hebrew and Yiddish Terms

Adonai	My Lord. Refers to Heavenly Father's greatness and glory in plural for emphasis. Used only in prayer and solemn religious services.
Aliyah	Al-EE-ah. Ascension. 1) Reading from *Torah*; or reciting a blessing over the reading during services, 2) Emigrating to Israel (generally referred to in English as making *aliyah*.
Amidah	(Ah-MEE-dah) Standing. A prayer that is the center of any Jewish religious ceremony.
Ashkenazic	From biblical term for Italy, Britain, Germany and France, Eastern Europe.
Berakhah	Benediction, blessing, praise, the unit of prayer.
B'nai Brit'h	Sons of the covenant. A worldwide fraternal order. Also a women's organization.
Bore Olam	A name for God. Creator of the world.
Brit Milah, Bris	(BRIT MEE-lah) Covenant of circumcision. The ritual circumcision of a male Jewish child on the 8th day of his life or of a male convert to Judaism. Frequently referred to as *bris*.
Bet tefilah, bet am, bet midrash, bet din	A house of prayer, a house of community, a house of study, a house of (court) order.
Chai	(KHI), Gutteral. Rhymes with Hi!) Life. Judaism is mainly concerned with this life and its relationships. The word is often used as a design on jewelry and other ornaments. Donations to charity are often made in multiples of 18, the numerical value of the word.
Challah	(KHAH-lah) A sweet, eggy yellow bread, usually braided, served on *Shabbat* and holidays.
Circumcision	See page 29.
Diaspora (dispersion)	Any place outside of the land of Israel where Jews live. Refers to the fact that Jews were dispersed from Israel by the Romans between 586 B.C. – 650 A.D.
El, Elohim, Elohenu	The name of God, emphasizing justice. *Elohenu* - our *Eloh*, our God. *Elohim* means "the gods", the plural of *El*, but always used with a singular verb. The One God as sum of all powers and justice.

En Sof	Infinite One. A name for Heavenly Father.
Gentile	A Gentile is anyone not descended from Abraham through lineage or baptism in the Church of Jesus Christ of Latter-day Saints.
Gesundheit	Health. A German/Yiddish word. When someone sneezes, wish them health.
Good Yontiff	gut-YON-tif. Good holiday. (Yiddish)
Goyim	The most commonly used word for a non-Jew is *goy*. The word "*goy*" is singular. "*Goyim*" (plural) means "nation," and refers to the fact that goyim are members of other nations, that is, nations other than the Children of Israel. There is nothing inherently insulting about the word "goy." In Exodus 19:6, God says the Children of Israel will be "a kingdom of priests and a holy nation," a *goy* ka*do*sh.
G-d L-rd	Abbreviated form of referring to Deity. The words are "GOD" and "LORD". They are holy to Jews in final form. Any written communication using full spelling is considered sacred.
Haggadah	(hah-GAH-duh) The book read during the Passover *seder*, telling the story of the holiday.
Halakhah	(hal lakh CHA) Jewish law. The complete body of rules and practices that Jews are bound to follow, including biblical commandments, commandments instituted by the rabbis, and binding customs.
Hallel	Psalms 113-118.
Ha-Shem	(hah SHEM) The Name. "*ha-Shem*" is often a substitute for God's name.
Ha-Tikvah	The Hope. The anthem of the Zionist movement and the state of Israel.
Hebrew	Language closest to Adamic. The name comes from the time of Avraham. His tribe of wanderers were called Eber, meaning "people of the other side". The name evolved.
Hosanna Shout	Originated in *Rosh Hashonah traditional prayers. Means "save us".*
Jew	The name indicates first of all a person from the kingdom of Judah. To be Jewish means to be of Semitic origin. Now, a person is a Jew if their mother is Jew, regardless of religion or other consideration.

Kaballah, cabala	Tradition. Refers to a book of mystical Jewish writings about many subjects including messianic thoughts and philosophy dating from the middle ages. See glossary of *People of The Book* by this book's compiler.
Kibbitz	To visit, gossip, converse lightly.
Kibbutz	Cooperative settlement in modern Israel, whose settlers hold all property in common.
Kosher	Please see Kosher, page 30, for description.
L'Chaim	(Le Khiam) To your health.
L'shanah tovah	(l'SHAN-ah tova) A good year. Don't <u>ever</u> wish a Jew a happy *Yom Kippur*. It is the Day of Atonement, the yearly observance of the Day of Repentance.
Malakh	Angelic messenger. Prayers are made only to God but we may converse with angels.
Mazeltov	(MA-zel-tov) Good luck.
Mensch	Gentleman
Menorah	The Temple candlestick *(Ex 25:8)*. Either a Sabbath or *Chanukah menorah*. The Sabbath *menorah* uses eight candles. Nine are used for *Chanukah*. One candle is called the *shammas*, or servant and is lit first and used to light the others. The *menorah* symbolizes the salvation of God *(Isa. 62:1)* and is considered God's lamp *(1Sam 3:1-3)*.
Meshuggah	Crazy, wild, foolish.
Mezuzah	(me-ZU-zah) Small cylindrical object containing miniscule scripture citations from Deut 6:4-9, 11:13-20. A blessing is recited before affixing the *mezuzah*. The *mezuzah* should then be affixed to the upper third of the doorpost on the right side as one enters the house or room. If the doorpost is wide enough to permit, the *mezuzah* should be tilted with the upper part slanting inward toward the house or room.
Minyan	(MIN-yahn) The quorum necessary to recite certain prayers; ten adult Jewish men.
Mitzvah	(MITS-vah) plural: Mitzvot (mits-VOHT) Commandment. Any of the 613 commandments that Jews are obligated to observe. It can also refer to any Jewish religious obligation, or more generally to any good deed.
B'rit hadashah	New Testament.

Ruach ha-Kodesh	Symbolizes the essence of God. *(Isa. 63:10, Psalm 51:13)*. **Like the Holy Ghost or Spirit.**
Semite	Shem was one of Noah's three sons (Genesis 10) and was the forerunner of the Semitic races. The Semites originated in Southwest Asia.
Sephardim	Spanish, Portuguese, Moorish, Moroccan Jews. Language is Ladino.
Shabbat Shalom or *Gut Shabbas*	Peaceful Sabbath.
Shalom Aleichem	(sha-LOM al-le-CHEM) Peace and health be with you.
Sheckinah	The manifestation of the glory of God.
Shema	Jewish Creedal Prayer, said at sacred events and is to be on the lips of a dying person. "Hear, O Israel, the Lord our God, the Lord is One." First in Deuteronomy 6:4 and stated by Jesus as the first of all the commandments; see Mark 12:29.
Shlemiel	A foolish or clumsy person.
Shofar	A ram's horn. Used on high official occasions, and in Israel at start of *Shabbat*. See Religious Practices for more information.
Siddur	The standard song and prayer book used by most Jewish congregations.
Star of David	The Mogen Dovid. A six-pointed star, symbol of Israel. The star was carried on the shield of King David. It has come to represent the Jewish state and the Jewish people. During the Third Reich Jews were required to wear a yellow star in public shame for their Jewry and to alert the SS to their whereabouts.
Synagogue	Assembly. Jewish meeting house. Jews often refer to any synagogue as their temple. Equivalent to an LDS ward or branch. A quorum of 10 males, a *minyan*, is required to begin a worship service. A rabbi will be selected from the congregation or hired from an outside source; he is paid. All religious services take place there, except a *bris*. Not a temple.

Tallis / Tellit	A four cornered prayer shawl or robe. Striped at ends, across its width. Originally lamb's wool, folded over shoulders, like a long scarf. Tele = lamb. Placed over the head during solemn portions of prayer to shut out distractions. Tassels on the ends are called *tzizit*. Fringes have numerical equivalent of 500, the strings, 8, the knots, 5. Total is 613 commandments given the Hebrews by God in *Torah*. Worn in worship during day hours and symbolizes *mitzvots*. Orthodoxy wear small 4 cornered garments beneath their suits. Similar to LDS garment and robes in essential meaning.
Phylacteries, Frontlets	Worn only by men. A small leather container in form of cube containing several scriptural selections is attached to a leather strap and placed on left arm opposite heart. The remainder of strap is wrapped around the left arm and hand seven times. A second container is placed on the head, a visible sign of covenantal love that binds God and Israel. Worn on weekdays at services as reminder of God's nearness. *Deut. 6:4-9, 11:18-21*
Teshuvah	Repentance, return to God.
Todah	Thank you.
U'rim and Tu'mim	(oo-rim and to-mim). Lights and perfections (NOT yourum and thumum!). A physical device aiding in revelation. These were two precious stones fastened into the two rims of a bow (Mos 21:27). Avraham, Aaron, the priests of Israel and prophets of old as well as the Nephite prophets used this sacred device *(Abr 3:1-4, Ex 28:30, Lev 8:8, Num 27:21, Deut 33:8 Omni 1:20,21, Mos 8:13-19, 21:26-28, 28:11-20, Ether 4:1-7)*. Joseph Smith used it in translating the Book of Mormon and other revelations *(JS-H 1)*.
Yarmulke	(YA-mul-ka) Skullcap. The small round cap worn by Jewish men in synagogue, at home and in public, marking them as observant Jews. Outside, they may wear black hats over their *yarmulke*.
YHVH	The Tetragrammaton = YHVH (יהוה), the distinctive personal name of the God of Israel. This name is commonly represented in modern translations by the form "Jehovah," It is sacred and never pronounced. To a Jew it is the calling down of God from Heaven. It represents the essence of God's being. Because there are no vowels in Hebrew, this word becomes Jehovah when vocalized. There is no "J" in Hebrew. The initial "J" is read as "y" and the mid-word "v" being read as "w". B/V alternates in spelling, pronunciation. Jews don't associate YHVH or Jehovah with Jesus Christ, but with Heavenly Father.

| Yiddish | For centuries, Hebrew was not used. Yiddish was spoken by Jews in Diaspora (dispersion) from about 1500, really flowering in the 15th century. Words and linguistic adaptations come from several cultures; German, Romanian, Hebrew, Polish, Russian. It is often spoken by *Ashkenazic* Jews. (See Cultural Groups, page 37.) |

Character of Hebrew Writings

Hebrew has fewer words than English, but many more word roots. Some words have great variety of meaning, depending upon the context in which they are used. Hebrew verbs and clauses are unique as well. There are only two tenses: perfect and imperfect. These explain modes of action as complete or incomplete. Verbs are found in different stems, expressing varying modes of intensity. This lends the language a vivid style, being rich in imagery. Note some Hebraisms: A stubborn people are criticized for being "for backward, not forward", divided loyalties are described as being "a heart and a heart". God's anger is described as a "shortness of breath", or "redness of nostrils". Hebrew nouns can be used like adjectives: "a garden of beauty" or "a mountain of holiness", instead of "a beautiful garden" or "a holy mountain". Many of these word arrangements are reminiscent of their Aramaic background.

The psychology of the Hebrew bible and Old Testament is concrete and physical. Bodily organs stand for emotions. Distress and fear may be described as "my bones melted". Hebrew is also rich in metaphor and simile. Israel is described as a "wild heifer", a "crooked bow", and so forth. Use of word images abound as well. God is described in anthropomorphic terms: His eye, hands, arms, feet, etc. He has divine anger, sorrow and repentance.

It should be noted here that the Jews believe Moses saw God face to face on Mt. Zion (Ex 19). Moses as a prophet had that gift and revelation. But Jews, oddly, do not believe that God is a person with human attributes because they do not see how He can be omnipotent, omnipresent and omniscient, yet contained in a human body. How to explain the seeming confusion? In the Talmud is their answer: The Jewish doctrine of "Incorporeality" asserts that terms are *borrowed* from human creatures to assist in the understanding. Where is our soul? We do not know, but we know we have one. So it is with God's place in the universe. References to God's bodily parts are analogies in the Jewish mind of human attributes.

The Book of Mormon was, of course, translated into the King James idiom; a solemn, antique style that was right for its time and season. Though it states it was written "in the language of the Egyptians", there is no doubt that it includes many Hebrew idioms, words and syntactical patterns, as well as Semitic language construction. It leaves no doubt that it is an inspired book full of revelatory surprises.

Some Hebraisms include the frequent repetition of "yea", "and", and "yes". Also the use of "behold", and especially the phrase "it came to pass" and "I say unto you." In the Hebrew this would have been said "And it came to pass in those many days." (From the Hebrew "Hayah".) Several other indications of Hebraisms in the Book of Mormon are:

English	Hebraism	English	Hebraism
Stone altar	Altar of stones	Dark mist	Mist of darkness
Brass plates	Plates of brass	Iron rod	Rod of iron
Harshly	With harshness	Joyfully	With joy
Surely	With surety	Spiritually	In the spirit
Strongly	(be with) strength	Abundantly	In abundance
Go to Jerusalem	Go up to Jerusalem	He thought	He said in his heart

Chiastic Structures

According to author and scholar John W. Welch, chiasmus literary forms are originally Hebrew and date at least to the 8th-10th centuries B.C. in Isaiah and the Psalms. There are many in the New Testament as well, and in the Book of Mormon.

Chiasmus describes a form of poetry told in parallelisms where the second (and other lines) are inverted. That is to say, the last element is placed first and the first, last:

For *my* thoughts are not *your* thoughts
Neither are *your* ways *my* ways, saith the Lord. (Isa 55:8)

A chiasm in Hebrew may be expanded to include any number of terms and lines written in one order and then in the exact reverse order. In Hebrew there appears to be no end to the terms or ideas that can be employed. A common structure of lines expressing parallel and inverse parallel ideas is repeated below:

a.   And the Jews
b.   Shall have the words
c.   Of the Nephites
c.   And the Nephites
b.   Shall have the words
a.   Of the Jews

(*A portion of the chiasm in 2 Ne 29:13*)

There are many chiastic structures in the Book of Mormon. See Mosiah 3:18-19, 5:10-12, 1Ne 15:5-11, 17:36-39, 2 Ne 27:1-5, Alma 41:13-15 and Alma 36, to name a few.

Letters of the "Alefbet"

The Hebrew and Yiddish languages use the same alphabet. The picture below illustrates that, in alphabetical order. Note that Hebrew is written from right to left, rather than left to right as in English, so *Alef* is the first letter of the Hebrew alphabet and *Tav* is the last. It also does not have upper or lower case letters. The Hebrew alphabet is often called the "*alefbet*," because of its first two letters. The consonantal pairs "KH" and "CH" are pronounced with a throat-clearing sound. Final letters (specifically used at ends of some words) are also included. Note: This throat-clearing sound is used in the common greeting "*Shalom Aleichem*". The table below represents formal Hebrew. Cursive writing is quite different.

ז	ו	ה	ד	ג	ב	א
Zayin (Z)	Vav (V/O/U)	He (H)	Dalet (D)	Gimel (G)	Bet (B/V)	Aleph (Silent)
מ	ל	ך	כ	י	ט	ח
Mem (M)	Lamed (L)	Khaf (Kh)	Kaf (K/Kh)	Yod (Y)	Tet (T)	Chet (Ch)
ף	פ	ע	ם	ן	נ	ס
Fe (F)	Pe (Pf)	Ayin (Silent)	Samech (S)	Nun (N)	Nun (N)	Mem (M)
ת	ש	ר	ק	ץ	צ	
Tav (T/S)	Shin (Sh/S)	Resh (R)	Qof (Q)	Tsade (Tz)	Tsade (Tz)	

Each letter in the *alefbet* has a numerical value. There is a study known as *Gematria* that is devoted to finding hidden meanings in the numerical values of Hebrew words. For example, the number 18 is very significant, because it is the numeric value of the word *chai*, meaning life.

These values can be used to write numbers, as the Romans used some of their letters (I, V, X, L, C, M) to represent numbers.

100	ק	10	י	1	א
200	ר	20	כ,ך	2	ב
300	ש	30	ל	3	ג
400	ת	40	מ,ם	4	ד
		50	נ,ן	5	ה
		60	ס	6	ו
		70	ע	7	ז
		80	פ,ף	8	ח
		90	צ,ץ	9	ט

Alef through *Yod* have the values 1 through 10. *Yod* through *Qof* have the values 10 through 100, counting by 10s.

The number 11 would be rendered *Yod-Alef*, the number 12 would be *Yod-Bet*, the number 21 would be *Kaf-Alef*, the word *Torah* (*Tav-Vav-Resh-He*) has the numerical value 611, etc.

The only significant oddity in this pattern are numbers 15 and 16, which if rendered as 10+5 or 10+6 would be a name of God, so they are normally written *Tet-Vav* (9+6) and *Tet-Zayin* (9+7).

The order of the letters is irrelevant to their value; letters are simply added to determine the total numerical value. The number 11 could be written as *Yod-Alef*, *Alef-Yod*, *Heh-Vav*, *Dalet-Dalet-Gimel* or many other combinations of letters.

Law

Maimonides' 13 Principles of Faith
1. God exists
2. God is one and unique
3. God is incorporeal (has no body)
4. God is eternal
5. Prayer is to be directed to God alone and to no other
6. The words of the prophets are true
7. Moses' prophecies are true, and Moses was the greatest of the prophets
8. The Written *Torah* (first 5 books of the Bible) and Oral *Torah* (teachings now contained in the *Talmud* and other writings) were given to Moses
9. There will be no other *Torah*
10. God knows the thoughts and deeds of men
11. God will reward the good and punish the wicked
12. The Messiah will come
13. The dead will be resurrected

The Seven Laws of Noah

Jews believe the 613 commandments in *Torah* are for Jews in particular. They leave the Gentiles to follow the 13 less exacting rules of conduct known as the Noahide Laws. According to traditional Judaism, God gave Noah and his family only seven commandments to observe when he saved them from the flood. These commandments, referred to as the Noahic or Noahide commandments, are inferred from Genesis Ch. 9, and are as follows:

(1) to establish courts of justice; 2) not to commit blasphemy; 3) not to commit idolatry; 4) not to commit incest and adultery; 5) not to commit bloodshed; 6) not to commit robbery; and 7) not to eat flesh cut from a living animal.

The Noahic commandments are binding on all people, because all people are descended from Noah and his family. The 613 *mitzvot* of *Torah*, on the other hand, are only binding on the descendants of those who accepted the commandments at Sinai and upon those who take on the yoke of the commandments voluntarily (by conversion).

History

Families of Israel

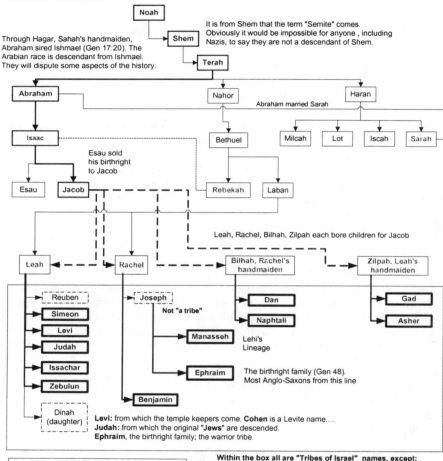

Through Hagar, Sahah's handmaiden, Abraham sired Ishmael (Gen 17:20). The Arabian race is descendant from Ishmael. They will dispute some aspects of the history.

It is from Shem that the term "Semite" comes. Obviously it would be impossible for anyone , including Nazis, to say they are not a descendant of Shem.

Noah
Shem
Terah
Abraham
Nahor
Haran
Abraham married Sarah
Isaac
Bethuel
Milcah
Lot
Iscah
Sarah
Esau sold his birthright to Jacob
Esau
Jacob
Rebekah
Laban

Leah, Rachel, Bilhah, Zilpah each bore children for Jacob

Leah
Rachel
Bilhah, Rachel's handmaiden
Zilpah, Leah's handmaiden

Reuben
Joseph
Dan
Gad
Simeon
Not "a tribe"
Naphtali
Asher
Levi
Manasseh
Judah
Lehi's Lineage
Issachar
Ephraim
Zebulun
The birthright family (Gen 48). Most Anglo-Saxons from this line
Benjamin
Dinah (daughter)

Levi: from which the temple keepers come. **Cohen** is a Levite name....
Judah: from which the original **"Jews"** are descended.
Ephraim, the birthright family; the warrior tribe.

Within the box all are "Tribes of Israel" names, except:
Reuben: lost his birthright; thus, not one of the "tribes of Israel".
Dinah: being female, not the name of a tribe.
Joseph: His sons are named tribes, not himself.

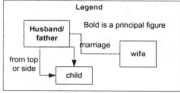

Legend

Husband/ father
Bold is a principal figure
marriage
wife
from top or side
child

Significant Judaic Scholars

Baal Shem Tov (the Besht, Rabbi **Israel ben Eliezer) (1700-1760 C.E.)** The founder of Chasidic Judaism. Although many books of his teachings exist, the Besht himself wrote no books, perhaps because his teachings emphasized the fact that even a simple, uneducated peasant could approach God (a radical idea in its time, when Judaism emphasized that the way to approach God was through study). He emphasized prayer, the observance of commandments, and ecstatic, personal mystical experiences.

Rabbi Nachman of Breslov (1772-1810 C.E.) The great-grandson of the Baal Shem Tov, Rabbi Nachman of Breslov (sometimes called Bratzlav, Breslau or Bratislava) was the founder of the Breslover Chasidic sect. Breslov is a town in the Ukraine where Rabbi Nachman spent the end of his life, but some say the name Breslov comes from the Hebrew *bris lev*, meaning "covenant of the heart." He emphasized living life with joy and happiness. One of his best-known sayings is, "It is a great mitzvah to be happy."

Theodore Herzl, (1860-1904). Founder of political Zionism. He was instrumental in helping Israel to become an independent nation. His disciples took up his work, especially Chaim Weizmann (1874-1952) who became the first president of Israel.

History of the Jews

There is no written history about the lives of the Hebrews in their homeland or about the Dispersion (*Diaspora*) from Babylon after about 430 B.C. but there are narrative histories from the period 170 B.C. to A.D. 70. These come from the works of Josephus (37 B.C.- A.D. 100) who was a priest in the rebuilt Second Temple, Herod's temple. He was a Pharisee and politically astute. He was of course not immune to bias or self interest or even selective ignorance, but his works are better than none at all.

Jewish history really began with the destruction of Jerusalem by the Babylonians in the period between 722 B.C. and 586 B.C. Through the eyes of the prophet Isaiah we read the warnings that were given the Israelites about their enemies, the Assyrians. It was at that time the name "Jew" really became their identity. Before that they were pre-exilic, pre-Babylonian Exile, not to be confused with the Exodus from Egypt back in 1500-1000 B.C., also known as the beginnings of the Iron Age. They were called Hebrews at that time. Some historians believe they fled before the Advance of the Hyksos, an Asiatic people who conquered Egypt in about 1650 B.C.

Some of them were Semitic, descendents of Shem, one of Noah's sons. They were wandering tribes from northern Arabia, around the area of the Tigris and Euphrates River valley. They were called the *Habiru*, *Hapiru*, or *Apiru*. Josephus tells us many of these people made an exodus from Egypt in about 1550 B.C. Some of the *Habiru* groups became the ancestors of the Arab people. The later chapters of Genesis appear to chronicle these times.

The Hebrews coalesced as a social order during this period, though there is no real history of them until the 13th century B.C. It is also possible the name came from the word "*eber*", to cross. This denoted those people who had crossed over from beyond the Euphrates. Our LDS Bible Dictionary does not apply dates to a sequence of events until after the death of Joshua and the period of the reign of Judges in Israel. It lists the start of Saul's reign as 1095 B.C. We read of his reign in 1 Samuel.

The fog really lifts by the eleventh century with the rise in the north of the kingdom of Israel and in the south, the kingdom of Judah, lasting until the eighth century. King David wrote many of the Psalms during his and Solomon's reign from 1000-925 B.C. The Hebrews at that time worshipped a primary god called *Yahweh*, which comes from the Hebrew letters YHVH, called the *Tetragrammaton*, a four lettered symbol which, according to the priests of the time, is a code for the actual name of God. They also paid homage to other gods who were public deities of the general Canaanite population.

That period was a time of radical change in the eastern Mediterranean area. Empires were broken down into city-states, ideographic writing gave way to syllabic script. The Greek and Hebrew alphabets were coming into everyday usage.

Babylon gave way to Persian rule in 500 B.C. Cyrus the Great allowed the Jews religious freedom and encouraged the rebuilding of their temple. He introduced the Aramaic language, which was to become to the Jews a language second to Hebrew. Persia eventually fell to Alexander the Great who introduced Hellenism the Jews to in 330 B.C., and that is where the apostles of Christ found them on their journeys around the Mediterranean in the first century A.D.

But the discourses of the prophets Amos and Hosea did a lot to change that. Yahweh dwelt on Mount Zion. They taught that Yahweh was no tribal god. He controlled the fate of humanity and ruled with justice, not mere whim. These Yahwist prophets, as they were called, came largely from the Judahite upper classes. They had Semitic names, meaningful names, like *Yehoyishma*=Yahweh will hear.

These prophets encouraged the Israelites to accept a declining interest in the worship of multiple gods. But during the reign of King Josiah in 609 B.C. the king of Babylon overthrew his Assyrian emperor and destroyed his city of Ninevah. We find our information on this war in the book of Jeremiah, who prophesied until after the downfall of Jerusalem under King Zedekiah.

In 586 B.C. Jerusalem was captured by Babylonian forces. The kingdom of Judah survived only two more decades. The Jews were deported to Babylon, but by then the religious life of the Judahites had become somewhat established as a monotheistic life. They gradually, in two major waves, returned to their homeland during the 5th and 6th centuries. It is from this period that the transformation of Israelite religion to Judaism is thought to have its most formative roots.

What are the most important events in Old Testament Hebrew history? Blessings from these seminal events resulted in numerous achievements in Jewish history:

The first Israelites of Avraham and Moses' time (circa 2000 B.C.) were descendants of nomadic Phoenician and Semitic groups wandering in the Levant area that surrounds the Mediterranean Sea, now consisting of Jordan, Syria, Turkey, Greece and Egypt.

Semites were of Caucasian blood. These people claimed descent from Avraham, Isaac and Jacob. They were the ancestors of the Hebrew people who were in the area of Israel during the time of the *Torah* writings.

The father of the Semitic people according to scripture was not Avraham but Shem, second son of Noah *(Gen 9:26, 10:21, Moses 8:12)* A great grandson of Shem, named *Eber (6 Gen 11:10-14)* may be where the name of *Hebrew* (colonist, colonizer, he who came from beyond or across the river) originated.

The ten "lost tribes (families) of Israel" who left Babylon following the Assyrian conquests there in 722 B.C. and 586 B.C. led to the scattering of the Israelites throughout the world. Some are the progenitors of the Anglo-Saxon (Saxon: from "Isaac's sons") tribes that gave rise to the Celtic (Keltic) peoples and their Druidic priests.

The Exodus 1500-1000 B.C. (1250 B.C. – the Greatest Exodus)
1. Moses transformed the liberation of slaves into the birth of a nation.
2. Formation of delegation of rule: Procedural law became model for English and US and French common law.
3. The monarch of King David, King Solomon, the erecting of temples.

4. Production of histories, psalms, messianic hope attached to Davidic line.

The destruction of Israel in 722 B.C.
1. The wandering and preservation of the ten tribes of Israel.
2. The destruction of Judah and exile to Babylon resulted in the formation of much of the Hebrew Bible.

The conquest of Jerusalem by the Romans in A.D. 70
Beginning of the foundation of classical, rabbi*nic* Judaism under the leadership of great rabbis. It also created a crisis of faith and the Sabbath became Israel's sanctuary.

The Moslem conquest of the Middle East in A.D. 640
Lead to philosophical and mystical inquiry that has become part of the Jewish religion and culture.

Events Affecting Early Jewish Thought and Movements
(Dates are approximate)

4000-3500 B.C. Sumerians in Babylon.

3000 B.C. Semitic tribes occupy Assyria, Phoenicians on Syrian coast

2500 B.C. Settlement of Aramaen nomads from Euphrates, Semitic Canaanites in Palestine

2000 B.C.. Hittites become kingdom, attack Syria

2100 B.C.. Avraham leaves Ur in Chaldees (Babylon)

1500-1000 B.C. Jews leave Egypt with Moses who receives the Ten Commandments

1400 B.C.. Founding of Rome

1100 B.C. Founding of London by Brutus of Troy

1002-B.C. Saul-king of Israel

1000-960 B.C. David, king of Israel and Judah

800-701 B.C. Celts move into England

753 B.C. Foundation of Rome

700 B.C. Isaiah's teachings, Celt settlement in Austria

705-68 B.C. King Sennacherib of Assyria defeats Egypt and Judah

722-586 B.C. Jewish Dispersions following Assyrian, Babylonian conquests

700-500 B.C. Start of Babylonian Captivity. Zoroaster founds Persian religion

629 B.C. King Josiah revives Judaism, renovates temple, finds first written manuscript of Deuteronomy

600-500 B.C. Nebuchadnezzar burns Jerusalem, Buddha is founder of Buddhism

600 B.C. – A.D. 421 Book of Mormon timeline- Early American civilizations, visit of the risen Christ

500-451 B.C. Start of Greek civilization in Rome

450-401 B.C. *Torah* becomes law of Jewish state

400-350 B.C. Pentateuch codified

336-323 B.C. Alexander the Great conquests enabled Hellenization of Asiatic, Semitic peoples

300 B.C.-A.D. 200 Thriving North African Jewish communities-trade, agriculture

301 B.C. Palestine reverts to Egyptian rule

285 B.C. Old Testament translated into Greek at Alexandria

168 B.C. Desecration of temple at Jerusalem, persecution of Jews by Antiochus IV

165 B.C. Temple rededicated by Judas Maccabeus-expels Syrians. Hasmonean siege

100 B.C. Writings portion of *Torah* completed by Gamaliel III. New synagogue practices installed

33-62 B.C. Paul's missionary travels and death. Thousands of Jewish conversions to Christianity

5 B.C. Greek translation-Septuagint-Old Covenant. Compiled by 70 Jews

7 B.C. (approximate) Birth of Joshua (*Yeshua*), Jesus in Nazareth

4 B.C. Herod the Great died

A.D. 30-37 Approx. dates of baptism, mission, death and resurrection of Jesus. Died in 22nd year of reign of Tiberius

A.D. 36 Most followers of The Way had left Judea

A.D. 66-73 Revolt of Zealots against Romans under Vespasian

A.D. 70 Titus, son of Vespasian ruled -Fall of Jerusalem, start of Christian expulsions

A.D. 70-132 Rabbi Johanan ben Zakkai, canonization of Jewish literature

A.D. 72 Fall of Masada to Roman forces. Defenders committed mass suicide

A.D. 79-81 Titus became emperor

A.D. 170-219 Rabbi Judah Hanasi Ordered Mishnah of *Talmud* written

A.D. 325 Council of Nicea

A.D. 350 Roman Catholicism

A.D. 383 Roman legions start to evacuate Britain

A.D. 400 Palestinian (Jerusalem) *Talmud* finalized

A.D. 500 Babylonian *Talmud* compiled for Diaspora Jewry

A.D. 600 Modern Hebrew formulated

Major Changes in History of Israel

(See *Timeline of Seminal Events in Modern Israel* below.) Jews through history have endured pogroms, purges, slavery, famine, death and conquering, rebuke of their rituals and the hatred of their conquerors, war and subjugation, disgrace, murder, fear, hopelessness, every horror known to mankind. Why? Read Romans 11. Yet the Jewish people continue to be the covenant people of God who remembers them and will fulfill his prophesies of restoration to them in these latter days.

2000 B.C. (approx) Abraham's migration to Canaan from Ur (Gen 11:31.)

1280 B.C. Freed from Egypt and Moses taught.

722 B.C. Assyrians - under King Hezekiah destroyed kingdom of Israel, later Judah

598-586 B.C. Babylonians conquered Judah

444 to 397 B.C Babylonians destroyed Temple from time of Ezra

336-323 B.C. Alexander - Greece -

312-364 B.C. Seleucids, part of Greek dynasty

37-4 B.C. Hasmonean domination through Roman conquerors, Pompey, Herod, Florus

A.D. 64 -70 Christian persecutions, Vespasian

A.D. 70 Fall of Jerusalem to Rome

A.D.73 Massacre at Masada - 967 Jews committed suicide

A.D.570-632 Arabs, Islam, Persian influences.

5th century Spanish Visigoth invasion. Massacre of Sephardic Jews

12th century British persecution of Jews relating to "blood libel" deaths

14th + 15th century Spanish inquisition: Christian baptism or death

15th century Moors expelled, then rest of Spanish Jews - expelled from Spain by King Ferdinand and Queen Isabella.

WW1 Ottoman empire - Turks overruled Islamic Jews, destroying their culture

1920 British mandate in Jerusalem

1940-44 German 3rd Reich - Hitler

1939-45 Russian purges in Poland, Russia

1970s Arab-Palestinian wars

1948 State of Israel

1948 – present Palestinian uprisings and land grabbing

1966 6 day war

Timeline of Seminal Events in Modern Israel

1918 British General Edmund Allenby defeats the Ottoman Turks and occupies all of Palestine

1920 Britain receives League of Nations mandate over Palestine at San Remo Conference and is told to facilitate creation of a Jewish homeland there.

1922 Church White Paper reduces British commitment to the Jewish people and gives 77 percent of area designated for them to Abdullah and the Arabs (Transjordan).

1929 Arabs riot in Jerusalem and massacre Jews in Hebron and Safed. Second White Paper further reneges on Britain's Jewish commitment and limits Jewish immigration.

1934 To flee Hitler, Jews try to immigrate. Britain refuses them entry. During following two years, 65,000 Jews immigrate to Israel.

1937 Peel Commission recommends partitioning remaining 23 percent of land designated for Jews, into two countries: one Jewish, one Arab.

1947 UN partitions Palestine into two states: Arab and Jewish. Arabs reject plan; Jews accept.

1948 Ben-Gurion declares independence. US President Harry Truman recognizes the new State of Israel. A year-long war of independence ensues when five Arab nations attack Israel.

> *Yom Ha-Atzmaut* is the celebration of Israeli Independence Day, marking the establishment of the modern state of Israel in 1948. It is observed on the 5th of *Iyar*. According to some views, the restrictions of the Omer period are lifted for this day. A few anti-Zionist Jews observe this day as a day of mourning for the sin of proclaiming the state of Israel without the Messiah.

1948-51 almost 700,000 Jews migrated to Israel.

1955-57 two-thirds of the almost 250,000 migrant Jews went to Israel (from Morocco, Tunisia, Egypt, Poland and Hungary).

1961-64 half of a further 450,000 migrant Jews went to Israel .

1961-62 virtually all Jews left Algeria for France.

1964 Fatah forms, with Yasser Arafat as its leader.

1967 Six Day War (June 5-10). Israel captures Sinai and Gaza Strip from Egypt, Golan Heights from Syria and the West Bank and East Jerusalem from Jordan. Israel reunites Jerusalem and assumes control of the Temple Mount. UN adopts Resolution 242.

1980s in two campaigns, Operation Moses and Operation Solomon, virtually the entire Jewish community of Ethiopia was airlifted to Israel.

1989-91 From the area of the former Soviet Union, some 400,000 Jews went to Israel, and many others went elsewhere in the West.

1992-93 most of the remnant of the Jews in Yemen left the country, many eventually reaching Israel. (From collected statistics of various sources)

1973 On Yom Kippur Soviet-backed Egypt and Syria attack Israel. US airlifts supplies. UN passes Resolution 338.

1977 Menachim Begin becomes Israeli Prime Minister and supports keeping disputed territories.

1979 Camp David Accords signed between Egypt and Israel.

1988 PLO recognizes Israel, renouncing terrorism. Yitzhak Shamir elected Israel's Prime Minister.

1991 Gulf War. Iraqui Scud missiles attack Israel. US deploys Patriot missiles to help Israel.

1992 Yitzhak Rabin becomes Israel's Prime Minister.

1995 Rabin assassinated. Shimon Peres becomes acting Prime Minister. Expansion of Palestinian rule in West Bank.

1996 Palestinians elect Arafat president. Netanyahu elected Israeli Prime Minister. Hamas detonates bus bomb killing 19.

1999 Israel elects former General Ehud Barak as Prime Minister.

2000 Barak, Clinton and Arafat meet. Palestinians initiate riots after Ariel Sharon legally visits Temple Mount. Violence and terrorism mount and continue. Called the Oslo War after the Oslo water rights agreements.

2001 Ariel Sharon elected Prime Minister. Suicide bombers and Islamic Jihad bombs kill many.

2002 More suicide bombings. Israel mounts Operation Defensive Wall. Arafat signs PA transitional constitution to guarantee Palestinian rights. It contradicts Arafat's "democratic, secular state" UN speech.

2003 Mahmoud Abbas elected Palestinian Prime Minister. Arafat maneuvers to maintain control. Violence continues. US releases Road Map peace plan.

Holocaust (Hebrew: Shoah)

> *"Yea, and ye need no longer hiss, nor spurn, nor make game of the Jews, nor any of the remnant of the house of Israel; for behold, the Lord remembereth his covenant unto them, and he will do unto them according to that which he hath sworn. Therefore ye need not suppose that ye can turn the right hand of the Lord unto the left, that he may not execute judgment unto the fulfilling of the covenant which he hath made unto the house of Israel." (3 Nephi 29:8-9)*

Jews in hiding were shot on the spot.

Hitler's rise to power was the initiation of a period that wrought great fear and destruction. Millions were forced to live in ghettos, only to be deported later to the concentration camps. The tragic details remained obscure until the liberation of the death camps and the further revelations during the Nuremberg War Trials. From the rise of the Nazi party in 1933 to the end of World War II in 1945, a diverse group was imprisoned, including Jews, Jehovah's Witnesses, Gypsies, dissenting clergy, homosexuals, as well as others who were denounced for making critical remarks about the Nazis. More than 6 million Jews perished. The area of devastation included all the countries Hitler's army invaded, including Germany itself.

Dachau, one of the first Nazi concentration camps, opened in March 1933, Six death or extermination camps were constructed in Poland. These so-called death factories were Auschwitz-Birkenau, Treblinka, Belzec, Sobibór, Lublin (also called Majdanek), and Chelmno The primary purpose of these camps was the methodical killing of millions of innocent people. Hitler had several camps built in 1935. In the beginning of the systematic mass murder of Jews, Nazis used mobile killing squads called *Einsatzgruppen.* The *Einsatzgruppen* consisted of four units of between 500 and 900 men each which followed the invading German troops into the Soviet Union.

By the end of 1943 the Germans closed down the death camps built specifically to exterminate Jews.

The approximate death tolls for the camps are as follows: Treblinka, (750,000 Jews); Belzec, (550,000 Jews); Sobibór, (200,000 Jews); Chelmno, (150,000 Jews) and Lublin (also called Majdanek, 50,000 Jews). Auschwitz continued to operate through the summer of 1944; its final death total was about 1 million Jews and 1 million non-Jews. Allied encirclement of Germany was nearly complete in the fall of 1944. The Nazis began dismantling the camps, hoping to cover up their crimes. By the late winter/early spring of 1945, they sent prisoners walking to camps in central Germany. Thousands died in what became known as death marches. *(From A Teacher's Guide to the Holocaust, University of South Florida.)*

Also known as Holocaust Remembrance Day, Yom ha-Shoah is a relatively new holiday. It occurs on the 27th of Nisan. "*Shoah*" is the Hebrew word for the Holocaust. This is a memorial day for those victims.

The Great Apostasy: Glorification of The Profane

Notational Outline Of Changes to True Church - A.D.100 - 1820

Apostasy: Abandonment of what one has believed in.

To Profane: To show irreverence for sacred things. To debase.

There have been several apostasies: The universal flood in Noah's day when people were swept off earth because of their sinfulness. (2) The scattering of Israel from Babylon was second. (3) The Book of Mormon cites the record of the Zoramites and Nephites falling away from righteousness (4) Lehi's vision described the confusing mists of darkness that led people astray (1NE 8:23). But the blessings of continuous revelation were taken from the *world* during the Great Apostasy following the ministry of the first apostles of Christ.

Jesus and his apostles knew that the early Church would apostatize soon after the apostles were martyred. Jesus himself announced that the world would reject him, his followers, his doctrine, and his Church (2 Thes 2:3-4). This states that an apostasy **must** come before the second coming of Christ *(2 Tim 3:1-5,7. Also Matt 24, Mark 13, Luke 21)*. The early apostles set up the Church knowing it would have only a temporary existence.

Enoch was shown the Savior's birth in the meridian of time, his ministry, atoning sacrifice, and resurrection *(Moses 7:45–47, 55–57)*. Enoch then saw a period of darkness which followed the Savior's earthly ministry; a time of apostasy, when "the heavens [were] darkened, and a veil of darkness [covered] the earth;" a period of "great tribulations" (Moses 7:61). This occurred when nearly all of the apostles were killed within a few years following the Savior's crucifixion and, as Paul foretold, Church members turned away from the truth, unable to "endure sound doctrine" as "grievous wolves enter[ed] in... not sparing the flock" *(2 Timothy 4:3–4; Acts 20:28–30)*.

The Apostasy affected everyone because truths were progressively stripped away. They became unavailable to Jew and Gentile alike. Just as the Christians had to wait the restoration of the Gospel in America so they could worship freely with Constitutional protection, *the Jewish people have had to wait until these latter days when they would again be able to practice their faith in America without persecution.* They had to endure the persecution and murders of so-called Christian sects who no longer practiced the Gospel preached by Jesus and his apostles. Now that the teachings and practices of the original church of the Christ the Messiah (*Yeshua* the *Mashiach*) are restored and truth is available to all, the veil of darkness is lifted. All the spiritual truth that has ever been upon the earth is now available. Let ALL the families of Israel partake!

Overall Causes of The Apostasy

Christianity was considered an illicit religion—atheists and anarchists, cannibals, licentious.

- Persecution of believers in Christ, nullification of free agency.
- Introduction of vital changes in essential ordinances.
- Unauthorized additions to the ceremonies of the Church.
- Loss of leadership and priesthood succession broken.
- Loss/change of doctrine, misunderstanding of atonement.
- Loss of true scriptures, perverted and untrue, confusing, ideas of God, Christ and Holy Ghost.
- Emergence of the Imperial Church of Rome.
- Many books and versions, uncertain authorship.
- Innocent changes, nefarious changes, councils of men change rules, disregard for true principles.
- Lack of apostolic overview, no prophet or apostles to lead churches.
- Unauthorized elections of officers, missionaries chosen from tradesmen and sailors.
- Bishops' wars, many competing philosophies/doctrines.
- Greek-educated leaders dominate, Heretics suppressed
- Powerful bishops take positions. Order of true Church restructured with one man (bishop) in charge.

During the first three hundred years after the crucifixion of Christ the teachings of Jesus and apostles were: live with love toward your fellow men. During the Apostasy it was becoming more necessary to *compel* a person who did not follow the accepted form of Christianity to conform.

Causes of Apostasy: 1st century A.D.

- Collapse of the Church's headquarters in Jerusalem (A.D. 60-70).
- The Jewish Christian members fled to the mountains (principally to Jordan, especially Pella).
- The leaders of the Church in Jerusalem were dispersed on missions or went into hiding.

- Jews dispersed across the world.

- Language of the Church shifted almost completely to Greek or Latin with little Aramaic spoken.

- Death of the leaders chosen by Christ in pagan cities (Rome, Antioch, Alexandria, Ephesus, Athens, etc.).

- The martyred leaders were largely of Hebrew origin.

- They were well versed in *Torah* and the doctrinal settings in which Jesus spoke.

- The apostles tried to interpret the doctrine (apostolic epistles) but were eventually killed.

- Church leaders were chosen by vote of the people rather than appointment through revelation.

- Personal unrighteousness overtook correct doctrine (idolatry, jealousies, envy, arguments, immorality, etc.).

- Doctrinal corruption prevailed: False prophets prevailed. *(See 1 John 4:1-3.)*

Docetism. Belief that Christ did not actually come in the flesh. He was not immortal. The truth of the resurrection of Jesus was treated as hallucination.

Gnosticism. Belief in a secret knowledge that only some of the Church members knew, concerning an esoteric and somewhat fanciful account of the Creation and the Fall of Adam and Eve in the Garden.

Causes of Apostasy: 2nd-3rd centuries A.D.

- Tertullian, A.D. 190. Lawyer, philosopher. Baptized, became Church elder. He believed the Godhead to be a legal entity but that God was composed of a philosophical substance non-material. Also believed in a professional priesthood without divine authority.

- Christians eventually found themselves in a society of emperor worshippers. It was as a loyalty cult for getting support for the political state.

- Christianity had become a religion of local deities.

- Sacrifices were offered for the continuation of blessings.

- Authority was not transferred properly. Priesthood authority cancelled out.

- Teachings corrupted by personal bias. Premortal existence principle confused, denied.

- Establishment of leaders chosen by the people

- In most of the locations, new leaders were not trained in Hebrew ways—many had almost no knowledge of *Torah* writings.

- Hebrew religion and scriptures were depreciated and changed.

- These new leaders reverted to their own background to decide on what is true and ethical (Greek philosophies).

- Long prayers and ceremonial pomp, expensive vessels used for sacrament.

- Doctrine of the Church became "the philosophies of men, mingled with scripture."

- Rise of the "Church Fathers: [Papiyas, Polycarp (Smyrna), Justin (Palestine and Rome), Clement (Rome), Tertullian (Carthage), Dionysius (Corinth), Clement (Alexandria), Origin (Alexandria), Eusebius (Caesarea), Jerome (Constantinople)].

- All branches of Church had lost inspired teachings:

- Exorcism was used to assure the initiate was free of bonds of Satan.

- Rise of bishops as final authorities in Church.

Special Movements: Marcionism and Montanism. Based on problem of evil in the world and its relation to matter, or mysticism. Philosophical systems involved. No unity in the Church and no priesthood.

Marcion: Believed the Old Testament had no place in Christian church. Published a Bible containing the book of Luke and ten epistles of Paul. He said the creator of the world is not the Father of Christ nor the god of the Christians. He founded his own church when the Roman church excommunicated him.

Montanus: Wanted the Church to reform itself back to Jesus' teachings. Saw himself as prophet receiving revelation, preparing for Second Coming. Believed there was no second repentance or return to Church once a person accepted Christ and then had sinned.

The Apostles' Creed

Drawn up in the first or second century, this emphasizes the true humanity, including the material body, of Jesus, since that is the point that the heretics of the time (Gnostics, Marcionites and Manicheans) denied. *(See 1 John 4:1-3)*. The **Gnostics** held that the man Jesus did not become the bearer or instrument of the Christ until the Spirit descended upon him at his baptism, and that the Spirit left him before Jesus' crucifixion, so that the Spirit had only a brief and tenuous association with matter and humanity.

The Nicean (Nicene) Creed, A.D. 325

The council met to deal with the schism created by Arianism. The Arians wished to avoid the heresy of politician Sabellius who believed in a divine *monad* (indivisible unit) that, by expansion, projected itself as Father, Son and Holy Spirit. The Arians separated the Son from God entirely so that they believed he was a creature having a beginning. "There was when he was not." The Son was but God's first creation, yet out of nothing and hence has preeminence over the rest of creation. The Nicene Creed is the most widely accepted and used brief statements of the Christian faith. In liturgical Churches, it is said every Sunday as part of the liturgy. It is common ground to East Orthodox, Roman Catholics, Anglicans, Lutherans, Calvinists, and many other Christian groups. Many groups that do not have a tradition of using it in their services nevertheless are committed to the doctrines it teaches. This has been in use with minor variations since 1549.

Traditionally in the West, the Apostles' Creed is used at baptisms, and the Nicene Creed at the Eucharist (*aka* the Mass, the Liturgy, the Lord's Supper, or the Holy Communion). Eastern churches recognize only the Nicene Creed.)

Traditional wording approved by the Nicene Council which established it as a theological formulation.

Nicene Creed

I believe in one God, the Father Almighty,

maker of heaven and earth, and of all things visible and invisible;

And in one Lord Jesus Christ, the only begotten Son of God,

begotten of his Father before all worlds, God of God, Light of Light,

very God of very God, begotten, not made being of one substance with the Father;

by whom all things were made who for us men and for our salvation

came down from heaven, and was incarnate by the Holy Ghost of the Virgin Mary,

and was made man; and was crucified also for us under Pontius Pilate;

he suffered and was buried; and the third day he rose again

according to the Scriptures, and ascended into heaven,

and sitteth on the right hand of the Father; and he shall come again, with glory,

 to judge both the quick and the dead whose kingdom shall have no end.

And I believe in the Holy Ghost the Lord, and Giver of Live,

who proceedeth from the Father [and the Son];

who with the Father and the Son together is worshipped and glorified;

who spake by the Prophets. And I believe one holy Catholic and Apostolic Church;

I acknowledge one baptism for the remission of sins;

and I look for the resurrection of the dead, and the life of the world to come. AMEN.

Essential points of Nicene Creed:

- Jesus was begotten from the substance of Father but it is a mystery how invisible immaterial substance can exist.
- God has no spatial dimension and is without spatial location.
- God is nowhere in particular but everywhere in general.
- He had not existed prior to time and time was not something he created and he was not concerned with it.
- He was very much involved with the temporal world.
- Mortals live inside of created time and have material bodies that fill space, but their god does not.

A revised Creed was approved by the Council of Constantinople (A.D. 381). An expansion and revision of the earlier Creed of Nicea with which it is often confused. This is the creed recited in many Protestant churches. The council met to refute **Apollinarianism.** This view saw Jesus as a combination of a divine Logos spirit, a sensitive human soul and a human body without a human spirit. These views were based on the platonic tripartite view of human nature. The council condemned this view in order to show that Christ, as truly human, could redeem the whole person.

The simple principles of the gospel were mixed with the pagan philosophical systems of the day.

Trinitarianism resulted in the writing of the Nicene Creed; declared false opposition of body and spirit, creating excessive asceticism. Church rituals were changed and added to in unauthorized ways; simple early Christian rites were replaced by complex pagan-influenced ceremonies. Baptism by immersion was lost; the baptism of infants was introduced [cf. Moro. 8] and communion was changed. The Church organization was altered. The apostles and prophets who were and are the necessary foundation of the Church of Christ, were martyred. This left a void that could not be filled by bishops; thus the medieval Church showed little similarity to the organization or practices of the New Testament Church.

Causes of Apostasy: 4th Century A.D.

- Introduction of images, pictures, effigies. Superstitious reverence for early martyrs. Pilgrimages to their tombs said to be protection against malign spirits. Idea of purgatory introduced.

- Baptism was changed to twice yearly at festivals in second century. Immersion done away with and sprinkling allowed. Baptism of infants performed as soon as possible after birth.

- Infractions of Church regulations brought fines, imprisonment, bodily torture and death. Gave rise to supererogation, the selling of pardons by priests. Purchasing remission of sins with money. The Pope assumed to remit sins in mortality so that in the hereafter there would be no punishment. All who opposed were accused of blasphemy. Private confessions to priests begun, penance performance for sin introduced with recitation of formulaic rituals.

- Scriptures not for the use of the laity, but only for teachers. Man-ruled papacy created which was tyrannical and without regard to moral restraint.

- **Athanasian Creed** (ca. A.D. 500). C A chief spokesman for the full deity of Christ was Athanasius, deacon of Alexandria, assistant (and later successor) to the aging Alexander. The fullest statement of the Trinitarian faith in abstract metaphysical terms. Essential idea is as follows:

> Essence: Each persona of the Trinity is fully divine, each is unique to itself, each is within the other, in perpetual intercommunication and motion, coequal and coeternal. A damnatory clause was included for those who did not accept this teaching.

Inquisition in Spain, end of 15th century. Secret tribunal for detection and punishment of heresy. Hundreds of thousands burned at stake.

The true Reformation seriously began in 1517. Power of the Catholic Church wanes as the Magna Charta of 1215 declares Church of England free. Eventually power of papacy waned. Between 12th-15th centuries, movements rose to reform church practices. The Renaissance brought reforms, revivals in learning and in New Testament and Humanism became popular through Erasmus.

Martin Luther. An Augustinian priest. Opposed sale of buying indulgences for sins not yet committed. Translated most of Bible into German. Rejected doctrine of oral confession and penance assignment. Said priesthood was power God bestowed on <u>all</u> baptized people. Argued that Protestantism placed responsibility of each Christian toward God. He adopted Nicene Creed. Stressed salvation by faith and grace alone. Condemned clerical abstinence, monasticism. He elevated marriage, wanted New Testament available to everyone.

Martin Luther was intensely anti-Semitic. In 1543 he wrote of the Jews: "...their synagogues should be set on fire, and whatever does not burn up should be covered or spread over with dirt so that no one may ever be able to see a cinder or stone of it. Jewish homes should be... broken down or destroyed." Jews should then be put "under one roof, or in a stable, like Gypsies, in order that they are not masters in our land... and put to work... by the sweat of their noses." His advice was typical of the anti-Jewish venom of his time.

Transubstantiation idea introduced and adopted during 1600's. Bread and wine were considered the actual blood and body of Christ in Roman Catholic Church. Emblems themselves considered divine. Men worshipped them. Also sometimes gave bread alone. Luther changed it to *con*substantiation, saying Christ's matter and blood became associated with the bread and wine.

Zwingli in Switzerland preached against celibacy, believed in long sermons, daily mass made educational, not mystical, Church services, pagan fixtures removed. **John Calvin** in Geneva spearheaded the Geneva Bible, said all other scriptures should be abolished. Accepted dogma of original sin and infant baptism. Stressed individual responsibility for conduct. New sects and practices began. Rise of the Methodists, Adventists, Baptists.

John Wesley, 1703-1791, Methodism. Also **John Knox** and in America and **Roger Williams** were prominent Reformation preachers.

English Reformation. Seemed to hold to higher moral standards than other Churches. Bishops were not political rulers. Henry 8th refuted Luther He wanted to separate the English Church from Rome. Ordered litany sung in English. Abolished oral confession, purgatory, dissolved monasteries, approved marriage. Humanism a major force in guiding English Church and kings toward Protestantism Episcopal beliefs based on 1571 Articles of Religion. Book of Common Prayer referred to God's love, forgiveness, anger, mercy, kindness. England keeps middle road between Catholicism and Episcopalianism. Communion practice varies from transubstantiation to spiritual presence. Broad view of grace, election, predestination. Protestants placed stress on responsibility of each Christian toward God.

The Prophet Joseph Smith in his First Vision (1820), was told by our Savior, Jesus the Christ, that all existing churches had gone astray both in their teachings and in their practices, although they had "a form of godliness" (JSH 1:18–19). Thus it was necessary for a "restoration" of the gospel to take place. See JST 2, Thes 2: 1-9.

After the Reformation, the Prophet Joseph Smith sought knowledge from the only source from which it could come—God. Men had forsaken the whole gospel system—its laws, ordinances, saving truths. Through the Book of Mormon, the Doctrine and Covenants, the Pearl of Great Price and latter-day prophets, those truths, insofar as they have been given, are being restored to the earth through our Lord's Church.

LDS Perspectives

Orson Hyde Prayer – Excerpts

LDS students know of the Orson Hyde Prayer in Israel. Orson Hyde ascended the Mount of Olives in 1841, built an altar to the Lord and offered a dedicatory prayer. This prayer is greatly appreciated by those Jews who know of it. Teddy Kolleck, a former mayor of Jerusalem, had a copy of the prayer in his possession when asked about the Israeli approval of BYU Jerusalem. There is a memorial to that prayer, an unusual thing for the Israelis to approve. *(1Kings 8:41-43 for a prophecy of Elder Hyde's visit)*

"Thy servant ...has safely arrived in this place to dedicate and consecrate this land unto Thee, for the gathering together of Judah's scattered remnants, according to the predictions of the holy Prophets—for the building up of Jerusalem again after it has been trodden down by the Gentiles so long, and for rearing a Temple in honor of Thy name...

"O Thou, Who didst covenant with Abraham, Thy friend, and Who didst renew that covenant with Isaac, and confirm the same with Jacob with an oath, that Thou wouldst not only give them this land for an everlasting inheritance, but that Thou wouldst also remember their seed forever. Abraham, Isaac, and Jacob have long since closed their eyes in death, and made the grave their mansion. Their children are scattered and dispersed abroad among the nations of the Gentiles like sheep that have no shepherd, and are still looking forward for the fulfillment of those promises which Thou didst make concerning them.

"Let the land become abundantly fruitful when possessed by its rightful heirs; let it again flow with plenty to feed the returning prodigals. Incline them to gather in upon this land according to Thy word. Let them come like clouds and like doves to their windows. [This was uttered before the airplane was invented.] Let the large ships of the nations bring them from the distant isles; and let kings become their nursing fathers, and queens with motherly fondness wipe the tear of sorrow from their eye.

"Let them know that it is Thy good pleasure to restore the kingdom unto Israel—raise up Jerusalem as its capital, and constitute her people a distinct nation and government, with David Thy servant, even a descendant from the loins of ancient David to be their king." (History of the Church, 4:456-57.)

At the close of each Seder meal on Passover (Pesach), the participants say "Next year, Jerusalem!" This shows their great fervor for the return and reconstruction of the Jewish people in their own land. The Prophet Joseph Smith, in a sermon on the second coming of the Lord said "Jerusalem must be rebuilt and Judah must return." *Smith, History of The Church, 5:337.*

Smith also prophesied the tribe of Judah will return to Old Jerusalem. Stephen D. Ricks, in his article *From Joseph to Joseph*, notes:

"The promise that Orson Hyde would be a watchman unto the House of Israel was fulfilled when, in April 1840, Joseph Smith assigned him to go to Jerusalem to dedicate Palestine for the return of Judah and the House of Israel... But unlike Christian expectations for the return of the Jews, (*his*) prayer did not include a prayer for affirmative preaching to them there. Back in 1854, the Prophet Brigham Young remarked that 'Jerusalem is not to be redeemed by our going there and preaching to the inhabitants. It will be redeemed by the hand of the Almighty... when the Savior visits Jerusalem and the Jews look upon him, and see the wounds in his hands and in his side and in his feet, they will... acknowledge him.'

"The importance of Hyde's mission lies in the realization of Abrahamic covenant promises. The mission of Orson Hyde to dedicate Jerusalem and Palestine for the return of the Jews to their homeland was fulfillment of the covenant promise made to Abraham, renewed with Isaac, and confirmed with Jacob 'that thou wouldst not only give them this land for an everlasting inheritance, but that thou wouldst remember their seed forever,' as Orson Hyde expressed it in his prayer." *Stephen J. Ricks, From Joseph to Joseph,* in Covenant and Chosenness in Judaism and Mormonism, p.99. Ed. Jospe, Madsen and Ward, 2001.

To Judah from Joseph: Ezra Taft Benson

Selections *from A Message to Judah from Joseph, by* President Ezra Taft Benson to Mormons, Non-Mormons, and Jews, in Calgary, Alberta, Canada, May 2, 1976

"My brethren and sisters—I use that as an inclusive greeting to all assembled, for it is a part of my faith that we are all children of one Father. To our Jewish friends I say, "Shalom Haverim," which is to say, "Good evening, brothers." It is a privilege and honor to be with you tonight.

Among some of my most cherished experiences and recollections are the fond association I have enjoyed in past years with the Jewish people in the United States and the land of Israel....

... We spent an evening with Ben-Gurion and his wife in their apartment in Tel Aviv. Most of the time was spent in the library, where there were

books from the floor to the ceiling on three walls. During the evening he said, "I want you to pray to God that he'll spare me for a few more years. I'm writing a history of the Jewish people, and it will take time to finish it." As we were leaving at the door that evening, he said, "You know, there are no people in this world who understand the Jews like the Mormons."

Yes, there is a great affinity for the Jews by the Mormons. The Jews have endured great persecution and suffering. This we understand, for our people have also undergone severe persecution and extermination. Indeed, the man we revere as a modern prophet, Joseph Smith, was martyred for his testimony in 1844. In 1846 our people had to exodus from the United States because of the threat of annihilation. We settled in a desert region similar to the topography around the Dead Sea and the Sea of Galilee. There we have developed our "land of promise."

Yes, we can empathize with the suffering of the Jews, for we have co-suffered with them. But our affinity toward modern Judah is not prompted merely out of mutual suffering; it is prompted out of a knowledge of our peculiar relationships together—relationships which claim a common heritage. Jeremiah has prophesied that in the latter times "the house of Judah shall walk with the house of Israel, and they shall come together." (Jer 3:18.) My prayer is that because of evenings spent together like this one, this prophecy will come to be fulfilled. **We need to know more about the Jews, and the Jews ought to know more about the Mormons.**

Among the kindred doctrines of the Mormons and the Jews is our mutual belief in Jehovah, a God of revelation. We share a common belief in the Messiah who will come. We further hold reciprocal beliefs in prophets. We hold a common commitment to the return of the Jews to the "land of Jerusalem," in fulfillment of the words of the ancient prophets. There are many other doctrinal and social similarities.

We declare that secrets long since hidden through the ages have been revealed again through a prophet by the revelation of "a new and everlasting covenant" to Israel. That prophet's name was Joseph Smith. These are the words of his own testimony:

[***President Benson quoted the First Vision***]

From the very inception of this latter-day work, which claims to be a restoration of the covenants given by God to Abraham, Isaac, and Jacob, this Church has had a deep interest in the remnant of the house of Israel, the descendants of Judah. In 1836, the Mormons completed their first temple at Kirtland, Ohio. In the dedicatory prayer which was offered on that occasion, Joseph Smith petitioned the "Lord God of Israel.

"O Lord ...thou knowest that thou hast a great love for the children of Jacob, who have been scattered upon the mountains for a long time...

"We therefore ask thee to have mercy upon the children of Jacob, that Jerusalem, from this hour, may begin to be redeemed; and the yoke of bondage may begin to be broken off from the house of David; and the children of Judah may begin to return to the lands which thou didst give to Abraham, their father." (D&C 109:60-64.) This was said during the Passover season, March 27, 1836.

Our common heritage *goes back to Abraham, Isaac, and Jacob. God reiterated to Jacob the same promises which were given to Abraham, and then gave Jacob the new name of Israel. His posterity—all those who descended through his twelve sons—were known by this designation. They were variously referred to as the "house of Israel," "children of Israel," or "tribes of Israel." I emphasize that all of his posterity received the family name designation through the twelve sons. Today it has become common practice to identify only one of his twelve sons, Judah, with the family designation "Israelite" because they have maintained their separate identity.*

As you carefully read the forty-ninth chapter of Genesis, you will find that Jacob, or Israel, pronounced blessings on all his twelve sons. Each was given a peculiar and distinctive blessing. Time will only permit a consideration of the blessings to two of these sons, whose blessings were preeminent above the blessings of the others. I refer to the blessings pronounced on Judah and Joseph. May I read first the blessing pronounced on Joseph:

"Joseph is a fruitful bough, even a fruitful bough by a well; whose branches run over the wall: The archers have sorely grieved him, and shot at him, and hated him: But his bow abode in strength, and the arms of his hands were made strong by the hands of the mighty God of Jacob; (from thence is the shepherd, the stone of Israel:

"The blessings of thy father have prevailed above the blessings of my progenitors unto the utmost bound of the everlasting hills: they shall be on the head of Joseph, and on the crown of the head of him that was separate from his brethren." (Gen. 49:22-26.)

There are several points which we should note carefully about this blessing: **Joseph's posterity would be numerous; that is, he would be a "fruitful bough." His posterity or "branches" would "run over the wall." His descendants would be sorely persecuted,** *which is the meaning of the phraseology "the archers have sorely grieved him, and shot at him, and hated him. The blessings on Joseph's posterity were to prevail* "above the blessings of my progenitors unto the utmost bound of the everlasting hills."

The northern kingdom, Israel, was subsequently taken into captivity by the Assyrians 721 years B.C.E. (Before Common Era). The Old Testament contains no history of Israel, nor of Joseph's descendants after this date. Are we to believe that God's promises to Joseph were for naught, that the prophecy of his posterity being numerous, "running over the wall," being sorely persecuted, and going to the "utmost bound of the everlasting hills" would not be fulfilled?

Because of the division which occurred between the two kingdoms, the Lord made special provision that separate records were kept. The prophet Ezekiel spoke of these records in these words: "The word of the Lord came again unto me, saying, "Moreover, thou son of man, take thee one stick, and write upon it, **For Judah**, and for the children of Israel his companions: then take another stick and write upon it, **For Joseph, the stick of Ephraim**, and for all the house of Israel his companions: And join them one to another into one stick; and they shall become one in thine hand. And the sticks whereon thou writest shall be in thine hand before their eyes." (Ezek. 37:15-20.)

Where is the fulfillment of this important commandment? Who claims to have the record of Joseph today? The record of Joseph has been brought forth in this day to Joseph Smith by a messenger sent from God. That record is called the Book of Mormon, named after one of the seed of Joseph who abridged the records of his people. The record tells the account of a colony of Israelites, descended from Joseph, who left Jerusalem before its great destruction during the Babylonian siege under King Nebuchadnezzar. It tells how **these descendants of Joseph came "over the wall"**—a metaphoric expression which denoted a barrier to them. **That barrier was the great ocean between the continents of Asia and the Americas.** This record tells how they were guided by the hand of the Lord to the land of America, a land of promise to Joseph and his descendants, a land "of everlasting hills." It tells how Joseph's posterity became very numerous upon the land until they filled it with a mighty nation. All this was in fulfillment of Joseph's blessing! The Book of Mormon further records the destruction of this mighty civilization because of their departure from the commandments of the God of Israel.

The records of these people lay buried in the earth for centuries. Then in 1827, a heavenly messenger turned them over to Joseph Smith. They were subsequently translated from their ancient reformed Egyptian writing into the English language and were published to the world in the year 1830.

The Judean prophet Ezekiel had declared that these records were to be "one in thine hand." I witness before you the fulfillment of that prophecy—the record of Judah in one hand, the record of Joseph in the other—one in our hands today.

I remember standing on the ruins of what was the largest Jewish ghetto in Europe in the Jewish section of Warsaw, Poland, in August 1946. There we were given a description of what had transpired as being somewhat typical of that which had gone on in various parts of Europe through the establishment of the medieval ghetto.

Here 250,000 descendants of Judah had lived prior to the war. Under the Nazi rule, through forced labor, Jews were required to build a wall around the ghetto. Later some 150,000 Jews from other parts of Europe were brought into that area. The Germans first tried to starve them out, but when that did not work, they transported over 310,000 Jews to the extermination camps. When Himmler found that there were still some 60,000 Jews alive in the ghetto, he ordered their "resettlement." When they forcibly resisted, the German S. S. General Stroop ordered the tanks, artillery, flamethrowers, and dynamite squads on the ghetto. The extermination which was to have taken three days lasted four weeks. The final report by the general read, "Total number of Jews dealt with: 56,065, including both Jews caught and Jews whose extermination can be proved." This report left 36,000 Jews unaccounted for which were no doubt claimed by the gas chambers. William L. Shirer, The Rise and Fall of the Third Reich.

I have visited some of the concentration camps, the mass graves, and the crematoriums where, it is estimated, six million of the sons and daughters of Judah lost their lives, reducing their world population from seventeen to eleven million I have been impressed to tears as I visited some of these wanderers, those persecuted and driven sons of our Heavenly Father, my brethren of Judah. Yes, the prophecies regarding the dispersion and suffering of Judah have been fulfilled. But the gathering and reestablishment of the Jews was also clearly predicted.

This predicted gathering has three phases: the gathering of Israel to the land of Zion, the American hemisphere; the return of the Ten Tribes from the north countries; and the reestablishment of the Jews in Palestine which had been long ago predicted by the prophets in these words:

"It shall come to pass in that day, that the Lord shall set his hand again the second time to recover the remnant of his people. .. And he shall set up an ensign for the nations, and shall assemble the outcasts of Israel, and gather together the dispersed of Judah from the four corners of the earth."(Isa. 11:11-12).

"Behold, the days come, saith the Lord, that I will make a new covenant with the house of Israel, and with the house of Judah." (Jer 31:31.)

The Book of Mormon is no less explicit in its prophecy concerning Israel's and Judah's gathering from a long dispersion: *"And it shall come to pass that they shall be gathered in from their long dispersion, from the isles of the sea, and from the four parts of the earth; and the nations of the Gentiles shall be great in the eyes of me, saith God, in carrying them forth to the lands of their inheritance.*

Since 1948, the people of the world have witnessed a marvelous drama taking place before their eyes; and yet it is a miracle that has gone rather unnoticed and unappreciated. One of the greatest events in history is the literal gathering of the Jews to their homeland from *"the four corners of the earth."* It is, as Isaiah prophesied, *"a marvelous work and a wonder." (See Isa. 29:14.)*

Since that time, the nation of Israel has fought three wars, regained Jerusalem and the western wall (Wailing Wall), and Added the Golan Heights and much of the Sinai Peninsula to its territory.

We previously considered the blessing that Jacob, or Israel, pronounced on Joseph. Let us now consider the blessing pronounced on Judah: *"Judah, thou art he whom thy brethren shall praise: thy hand shall be in the neck of thine enemies; thy father's children shall bow down before thee. Judah is a lion's whelp: from the prey, my son, thou art gone up: he stooped down, he couched as a lion, and as an old lion; who shall rouse him up?*

"The sceptre shall not depart from Judah, nor a lawgiver from between his feet, until Shiloh come; and unto him shall the gathering of the people be. Binding his foal unto the vine, and his ass's colt unto the choice vine; he washed his garments in wine, and his clothes in the blood of grapes:

The great blessing to Judah is that it contemplated the coming of Shiloh who would gather his people to him. This prophecy concerning Shiloh has been subject to several Rabbinic and Christian interpretations and the object of considerable controversy. The interpretation given this passage by the Mormon Church is one based on revelation to modern prophets, not on scholarly commentary. It was revealed to Joseph Smith that Shiloh is the Messiah. *(See Gen. 50:24, JST)*

President Wilford Woodruff, the apostle who became the fourth President of the Church I represent, said this to the Jews in the year 1879:

"And this is the will of your great Elohim, O house of Judah, and whenever you shall be called upon to perform this work, the God of Israel

will help you. You have a great future and destiny before you and you cannot avoid fulfilling it; you are the royal chosen seed, and the God of your father's house has kept you distinct as a nation for eighteen hundred years, under all the oppression of the whole Gentile world. You may not wait until you believe on Jesus of Nazareth, but when you meet with Shiloh your king, you will know him; your destiny is marked out, you cannot avoid it ... the Gentiles may gather together their armies to go against you to battle but when this affliction comes, the living God, that led Moses through the wilderness, will deliver you, and your **Shiloh will come and stand in your midst and will fight your battles; and you will know him, and the afflictions of the Jews will be at an end, while the destruction of the Gentiles will be so great that it will take the whole house of Israel who are gathered about Jerusalem, seven months to bury the dead of their enemies,** and the weapons of war will last them seven years for fuel, so that they need not go to any forest for wood. These are tremendous sayings—who can bear them? Nevertheless they are true, and will be fulfilled, according to the sayings of Ezekiel, Zechariah, and other prophets. Though the heavens and the earth pass away, not one jot or tittle will fall unfulfilled." (Matthias F. Cowley, Wilford Woodruff, Bookcraft, 1964).

Christian history has emphasized the point that the Jews as a nation rejected their Messiah. **Overlooked has been the fact that many Jews did believe him to be the Messiah. Among those Jews who did so were most of the original twelve apostles and thousands of others who were converted during and following the Pentecost.**

You will recall the episode of Joseph and his brethren in the Old Testament, and how he was sold into Egypt. You will remember that, because of a famine in the land of Canaan, his brethren were compelled to go to Egypt to purchase corn from the granaries. Joseph had risen to the position of governor over the land, and was in charge of those granaries. One of the most touching scenes recorded in the Torah is when Joseph made himself known to his brethren: "I am Joseph your brother..." (Gen. 45:4.)

To you, our friends of modern Judah, we declare, "We are Joseph, your brothers." We claim kinship with you as descendants from our fathers, Abraham, Isaac, and Jacob. We belong to the same family. We, too, are the house of Israel.

In Jacob's blessing to Judah, he declared: "Judah is...as an old lion; who shall rouse him up?" (Gen. 49:9). We come as messengers bearing the legitimate authority to arouse Judah to her promises. We do not ask Judah to forsake her heritage. We are not asking her to leave father, *mother, or family. We bring a message that Judah does not possess. That message constitutes "living water" from the Fountain of living water.*

Our prophet, Joseph Smith, was given a commandment by the Lord to turn **"the hearts of the Jews unto the prophets, and the prophets unto the Jews."** *(D&C 98:17.) We are presently sending our messengers to every land and people whose ideology permits us entrance. We have been gathering Joseph's descendants for 146 years. We hope you, who are of Judah, will not think it an intrusion for us to present our message to you. You are welcome to come to our meetings. We display no crosses. We collect no offerings. We honor your commitment to your unique heritage and your individuality. We approach you in a different way than any other Christian Church because we represent the restored covenant to the entire house of Israel.*

As one who, by special assignment, has been given authority in the house of Israel today, I ask the God of Abraham, Isaac, and Jacob to bless my brethren of Judah and have mercy on them; that the land to which Judah has returned after a long night of dispersion shall be fruitful, prosperous, and become the envy to her neighbors; that the nation Israel shall be delivered from all her oppressors and enemies; that Judah will "draw water out of the wells of salvation" (Isa. 12:3) and fulfill all those prophecies that God declared through his prophets Isaiah, Ezekiel, and Jeremiah, even that prophecy through Zechariah that "the Lord shall inherit Judah his portion in the holy land, and shall choose Jerusalem again" (Zech. 2:12).

Relevant LDS Scriptural Citations

Avrahamic Covenant
1 Ne. 15:18 covenant with A. to be fulfilled
1 Ne. 17:40 (22:9 , 2 Ne. 29:14 , 3 Ne. 20:25,27, Morm. 5:20, Ether 3:11) God covenants with A
D&C 52:2 (86:9) the Lord's people are heirs according to the covenant;
D&C 84:34 they who magnify callings become seed of A.;
D&C 84:99 election brought to pass by faith and covenant of Israel's fathers;
D&C 110:12 Elias commits dispensation of gospel of A.;
D&C 124:58 through A. and his seed shall kindreds of earth be blessed;
D&C 132:32 do works of A
Abr. 2:9–11 promises given to *A.*

Assyria:
2 Ne. 21:11,16 (Isa. 11:11,16) the Lord to recover his people from *A.*

Blindness
2 Ne. 9:32 wo unto *b.* who will not see;
2 Ne. 27:29 (Isa. 29:18) b. shall see out of obscurity;
Jacob 4:14 Jews' b. came from looking beyond mark;
Jarom 1:3 much to be done among people because of b. of minds;
Mosiah 3:5 (3 Ne. 17:9; 26:15) the Lord will cause b. to receive their sight;
Mosiah 11:29 eyes of people were b.
Ether 4:15 veil of unbelief causes Israelites to remain in *b.*

Blood Shedding of
2 Ne. 10:6 because of Jews' iniquities, bloodshed shall come upon them
D&C 20:79 wine in remembrance of b. which Christ shed for men;
D&C 27:2 the Lord's b. was shed for remission of sin;
D&C 49:21 wo to man who sheds b. or wastes flesh without need;
D&C 58:52–53 (63:30–31) inheritances to be obtained by purchase and
    not by shedding of *b.*

Bondage
1 Ne. 17:25 children of Israel were in b.
1 Ne. 19:10 (Alma 29:12; 36:28) the Lord leads his people out of *b.* in
    Egypt;
Mosiah 7:15, D&C 103:17 Israel to be led out of *b.*; D&C 104:83–84

Branch
1 Ne. 10:12 Lehi[1] compares Israel to olive tree whose b. are broken off;
1 Ne. 10:14 (15:7, 13, 16) natural b. of olive tree to be grafted in;
1 Ne. 15:12 (19:24; 2 Ne. 3:5; 9:53; Alma 26:36) Jacob 2:25) the Lord
    would raise righteous *b.* from descendants of Joseph˙ Nephites;
1 Ne. 21:1 (Isa. 11:1) *b.* shall grow out of Jesse's roots;
Jacob 5:3–77 parable of natural and wild b. of olive trees;
Jacob 6:4 God remembers house of Israel, both roots and b.;
Alma 16:17 word preached among Nephites that as b. they might be
    grafted into true vine
D&C 10:60 (John 10:16) other sheep were b. of house of Jacob;

Captivity
1 Ne. 1:13 (10:3; 2 Ne. 6:8; 25:10; Omni 1:15) inhabitants of Jerusalem to
    be carried away c. into Babylon;
1 Ne. 5:10 Jews have been destroyed, except those carried c. into
    Babylon;
Omni 1:15 people of Zarahemla came from Jerusalem when Zedekiah
    was carried *c.* into Babylon.

Covenant
1 Ne. 13:23 book is record of Jews, contains c. of the Lord;
1 Ne. 15:18 (3 Ne. 15:8; 16:5, 11–12; 20:12, 25–27, 29; 21:7; Morm. 5:20; 8:23; 9:37; Ether 4:15; 13:11) c. made to Avraham to be fulfilled in latter days;
1 Ne. 17:40 the Lord c. with Avraham, Isaac, Jacob;
1 Ne. 17:40 the Lord remembered c. made to fathers and brought them out of Egypt;
1 Ne. 19:15 when Jews no more turn aside hearts from the Holy One, he will remember c. made to fathers;
1 Ne. 22:9 marvelous work among Gentiles shall make known the Father's c. unto Avraham;
1 Ne. 29:4 Jews are the Lord's ancient c. people;
1 Ne. 29:14 (3 Ne. 20:25, 27) the Lord c. with Avraham to remember his seed
D&C 1:15 (54:4; 104:4, 52) men have broken the Lord's everlasting c.;
D&C 1:22 (45:9; 49:9) the Lord will establish everlasting c.;
D&C 2:1 (sec. 132) old c. done away, the Lord gives new and everlasting c
D&C 49:9 c. was from beginning;
D&C 52:2 the Lord's people are heirs according to c.;
D&C 54:4 Saints' c. with the Lord has been broken;
D&C 54:6 they who keep c. will obtain mercy;
D&C 66:2 everlasting c. fulness of gospel;
D&C 76:69 (107:19) Jesus, mediator of new c.;
D&C 76:101 telestial heirs received not everlasting c.;
D&C 78:11 (82:11, 15) Saints to organize themselves by bond or everlasting c.
Abr. 2:9–11 the Lord's c. with Avraham.

Desolation
3 Ne. 22:3 (**Isa.** 54:3) Israel's seed shall make d. cities to be inhabited.

Destruction
1 Ne. 1:4 (7:13; 17:43; 2 Ne. 1:4; Hel. 8:20–21) Jerusalem must be d.
1 Ne. 14:7 hardhearted to be brought down to d., both temporally and spiritually;
1 Ne. 6:15 they that believe not in the Messiah shall be d.;
1 Ne. 10:6 (25:9) because of iniquities, d. shall come upon Jews;
1 Ne. 25:9 d. of Jews from generation to generation always foretold by prophets
1 Ne. 5:20 the Lord told people of d. of Jerusalem;
Moses 4:3 Satan sought to d. man's agency;

Dispersion

2 Ne. 10:8 (3 Ne. 21:1) Jews shall be gathered from long d.;

2 Ne. 21:12 (3 Ne. 5:26; Isa. 11:12) the Lord shall gather d. of Israel;

3 Ne. 21:26 work of the Father to commence among d. tribes;

Morm. 8:15 records to be brought forth for welfare of long *d.* covenant people.

Ephraim—kingdom of Israel

2 Ne. 17:8 (Isa. 7:8) E. to be broken that it be not a people;

2 Ne. 17:17 (Isa. 7:17) the Lord shall bring upon house of David days that have not come from day that E. departed from Judah;

2 Ne. 19:8–9 (Isa. 9:8–9) all people, even E., to know the Lord's word;

2 Ne. 19:21 (Isa. 9:21) Manasseh and E. shall be against Judah;

2 Ne. 21:13 (Isa. 11:13) E. shall not envy Judah, and Judah shall not vex E.

1 Ne. 5:14 (Alma 10:3) Lehi ... was a descendant of Joseph

1 Ne. 13:34 (3 Ne. 15:12) this remnant ... is the seed of thy father

1 Ne. 15:12 are we not a branch of the house of Israel

2 Ne. 3:5 branch which was to be broken off

2 Ne. 19:21 Ephraim, Manasseh, they together shall be against Judah

Jacob 2:25 righteous branch from the fruit of the loins of Joseph

Alma 46:23 (3 Ne. 10:17) we are a remnant of the seed of Joseph

Ether 13:6 New Jerusalem should be built ... unto the remnant of the seed of J

2 Ne. 29:13 shall have the words of the lost tribes of Israel

3 Ne. 15:15 concerning the other tribes of the house of Israel

3 Ne. 17:4 I go ... to show myself unto the lost tribes of Israel

3 Ne. 21:26 work ... commence among ... *tribes* which have been lost

Ether 13:11 gathered in from ... the north countries

1 Ne. 10:14 house of I. ... gathered together

1 Ne. 12:9 twelve apostles ... shall judge the twelve tribes

1 Ne. 21:6 to raise up the tribes of Jacob

Jacob 5:3 house of I. like unto a tame olive tree

JST Gen. 50:24–26; 2 Ne. 3; 29, D&C 27:5 the Lord has committed keys of record of stick of E. to Moroni2;

D&C 64:36 rebellious are not of blood of E.;

D&C 113:4 rod that should come from Stem of Jesse is descendant of Jesse and of E.;

D&C 133:30 lost tribes to bring treasures to children of E.;

Fold

1 Ne. 15:15 will they not come unto the true f. of God

1 Ne. 22:25 (3 Ne. 16:3) shall be one f. and one shepherd

2 Ne. 9:2 restored to the true Church and f.

D&C 10:59 other sheep have I not of this *f.*

Foundation
1 Ne. 13:4 among ... the Gentiles the f. of a great Church
1 Ne. 14:9 whose f. is the devil
Jacob 4:16 this stone shall become the ... only sure f. upon which the Jews can build
D&C 124:33, 41 (128:5) ordinances prepared before f. of world;
D&C 130:20 (132:5) law decreed in heaven before f. of world;
D&C 138:53 choice spirits reserved to lay f. of great latter-day work
Moses 5:57 the Son prepared from f. of world;
Moses 6:44 f. of earth is the Lord's;
Moses 6:54 children are whole from f. of world;
Moses 7:47 the Lamb is slain from f. of world;
Abr. 1:3 priesthood came down from before *f.* of earth to present.

Fruit
Jacob 5:26 (5:32, 46, 65) Pluck off the branches that have not brought forth good f. Fulfill
3 Ne. 9:17 (12:46, 15:5) In Christ is the Law of Moses fulfilled
D&C 45:25, 30 times of Gentiles to be *f.*;
D&C 56:11 these words shall be *f.*;
D&C 58:31 have I promised and have not *f.*;
D&C 58:33 some say the Lord's promises are not *f.*;
D&C 74:3 law of Moses was *f.*;
D&C 85:10 as the Lord speaks, he will also *f.*;
D&C 105:34 commandments concerning Zion and her law to be *f.*

Gather
2 Ne. 23:4 kingdoms of nations *g.* together
2 Ne. 29:14 Israel, shall be *g.* home unto the lands of their possessions, and my word also shall be *g.* in one
3 Ne. 10:6 (D&C 10:65; 29:2) *g.* you as a hen *g*
D&C 42:36 covenant people to be *g.* in one;
D&C 45:25 Christ prophesies to disciples that Jews will be *g.*;
D&C 45:43 remnant will be *g.* at the Lord's coming;
D&C 45:69 people to be *g.* unto Zion out of every nation;
D&C 45:71 righteous to be *g.* from among nations;
D&C 77:15 two prophets will testify to Jews after they are *g*
D&C 110:11 Moses commits keys of *g.* of Israel;
Moses 7:62 Enoch foretells *g.* of God's elect;
JS—M 1:27 *g.* of elect compared to *g.* of eagles to carcass;
JS—M 1:37 angels to *g.* elect from four winds;

A of F 10 we believe in literal *g.* of Israel.

Gentile
1 Ne. 13:25 go forth from the Jews in purity unto the *G.*
1 Ne. 15:13 gospel ... come unto the *G.,* and from the *G.* unto the remnant
1 Ne. 22:6 nursed by the *G.* set them up for a standard
2 Ne. 10:18 *G.* blessed and numbered among the house of Israel
Jacob 5:10 grafted in the branches of the *wild* olive tree
3 Ne. 15:22 *G.* should be converted through their preaching
Morm. 7:8 record ... unto the *G.* from the Jews
D&C 14:10 (19:27; 90:9; 107:33, 97) the Lord to bring forth fulness of
    gospel from *G.* unto Israel;
D&C 18:26–27 Twelve called to declare gospel, both to *G.* and Jew;
D&C 19:27 Book of Mormon is the Lord's word to *G.*;
D&C 35:7 there shall be great work among *G.*;
D&C 35:7 abominations of *G.* to be manifest;
D&C 42:39 the Lord to consecrate riches of *G.* unto poor of Israel;
D&C 45:9 *G.* to seek everlasting covenant;

Hardheartedness
1 Ne. 14:7 (Alma 13:4) *h.* of their hearts and the blindness of their minds
1 Ne. 18:20 nothing ... could soften their *hearts*
1 Ne. 22:5 against him will they *h.* their hearts
2 Ne. 6:10 after they have *h.* their hearts
2 Ne. 25:10 they *h.* their hearts ... have been destroyed
2 Ne. 33:2 *h.* their hearts against the Holy Spirit
Mosiah 3:15 they *h.* their hearts, and understood not
Mosiah 11:29 eyes blinded: therefore they *h.* their hearts
Alma 12:10 he that will *h.* his heart, the same receiveth the lesser portion
Alma 12:37 (34:31) let us repent, and *h.* not our hearts
Alma 24:30 they become more *h.,* and thus their state becomes worse
Hel. 6:35 Spirit ... began to withdraw ... because of the wickedness and the
    h. of their hearts
3 Ne. 20:28 if they shall *h.* their hearts against me I will return their
    iniquities
3 Ne. 21:22 repent ... and *h.* not their hearts
D&C 84:24 children of Israel hardened hearts and could not endure the
    Lord's presence;
D&C 84:76 men to be upbraided for evil hearts of unbelief;
Moses 6:27 hearts have waxed hard;
Abr. 1:6 hearts of Avraham's fathers were set to do evil.

Inheritance
2 Ne. 1:9 none ... to take away the land of their *i.*

2 Ne. 10:7 shall be restored ... unto the lands of their *i*.
Alma 5:58 unto them will I grant an *i*. at my right hand
3 Ne. 21:22 given this land for their *i*.
Ether 7:16 obtain the land of their first *I*
1 Ne. 17:41 the Lord straitened Israel in wilderness because of *i*.; 17:45
   (Mosiah 13:29; Alma 46:8; Hel. 12:4).

Iniquity Iniquitous:
2 Ne. 25:9 Jews have been destroyed from generation to generation
   according to I
D&C 45:53 Jews to weep because of i.;
D&C 101:11 God's indignation to be poured out when cup of i. is full
D&C 76:109 inhabitants of telestial world were i. as stars;
D&C 132:30 Avraham's seed to continue *i*. as stars.

Isaiah - Hebrew prophet:
Title Page (1 Ne. 12:9; 15:12; 2 Ne. 6:5; 3 Ne. 20:10; Morm. 7:2) Nephites
   and Lamanites are remnant of house of *I*.;
1 Ne. 10:12 (15:12; Jacob 5:3–6:1) house of *I*. compared to olive-tree;
1 Ne. 10:14 (15:12–18) house of *I*. to come to knowledge of true Messiah;
1 Ne. 12:9 (Morm. 3:18) twelve tribes of *I*. to be judged by Twelve
   Apostles;
1 Ne. 13:23 (14:5, 8, 17; 22:6, 9, 11; 2 Ne. 2 Ne 6:5 *i*. spake concerning all
   house of Israel;
2 Ne. 11:2 *I*. saw the Redeemer;
2 Ne. 9:1; 3 Ne. 16:5, 11–12; 20:12, 27; 21:4, 7; 29:3, 8; Morm. 5:20; 9:37;
   Ether 4:15; Moro. 10:31) covenants with house of *I*.;
1 Ne. 13:33–34 (19:11) the Lamb will visit remnant of house of *I*.;
1 Ne. 14:2 (2 Ne. 10:18; 3 Ne. 16:13–15; 21:6; 30:2) if Gentiles harden not
   hearts, they shall be numbered among house of *I*.;
1 Ne. 14:26 sealed writings shall come forth unto house of *I*.;
1 Ne. 15:14 (2 Ne. 28:2; 3 Ne. 20:10; Morm. 7:1) remnant of Lehites' seed
   shall know they are of house of *I*.;
1 Ne. 15:17 the Lord shall be rejected of Jews, or of house of *I*.;
1 Ne. 17:23 children of *I*. were led out of Egypt because they hearkened to
   the Lord;
1 Ne. 17:25 children of *I*. were in bondage;
1 Ne. 17:29 Moses smote rock, that children of *I*. might quench thirst;
1 Ne. 19:10 sign of Christ's death to be given house of *I*.;
1 Ne. 20:1 (Isa. 48:1) house of Jacob are called by name of *I*.;
1 Ne. 20:12 hearken, O Jacob, and *I*. my called;
1 Ne. 21:3 (Isa. 49:3) thou art my servant, O *I*.;
1 Ne. 21:7 (Isa. 49:7) the Lord, the Redeemer of *I*.;

1 Ne. 22:12 those who are of house of *I.* shall know that the Lord is their Savior, the Mighty One of *I.*;

1 Ne. 22:14 nations that war against house of *I.* shall be turned one against another;

2 Ne. 3:9 Moses raised up to deliver house of *I.*;

2 Ne. 6:5 (3 Ne. 23:2) Isaiah[1] spake concerning all house of *I.*;

2 Ne. 9:53 our seed shall become righteous branch unto house of *I.*;

2 Ne. 14:2 (Isa. 4:2) fruit of earth shall be comely to them that are escaped of *I.*;

2 Ne. 15:7 **(Isa.** 5:7) vineyard of the Lord is house of *I.*;

2 Ne. 18:14 (Isa. 8:14) he shall be for rock of offense to both houses of *I.*;

2 Ne. 19:8 (Isa. 9:8) the Lord sent his word unto Jacob and it hath lighted upon *I.*;

2 Ne. 19:12 (Isa. 9:12) Syrians and Philistines shall devour *I.*

Israel:

3 Ne. 16:7 because of unbelief of house of *I.*, truth shall come unto Gentiles;

3 Ne. 17:14 Jesus troubled because of wickedness of house of *I.*;

3 Ne. 21:20 unrepentant to be cut off from house of *I.*;

3 Ne. 20:11–12 when words of *I.* should be fulfilled, then is fulfilling of the Father's covenant with Israel;

3 Ne. 23:1 (Morm. 8:23) search these things diligently, for great are words of *I.*

3 Ne. 25:4 **(Mal.** 4:4) the Lord commanded law of Moses for all *I.*;

3 Ne. 29:1 covenant which the Father made with children of *I.* shall be fulfilled;

3 Ne. 29:2 ye need not say the Lord delays his coming to children of *I.*;

Morm. 5:10–11 Gentiles who have care for house of *I.* will have sorrow for calamity of house of *I.*;

Morm. 8:21 he who breathes out wrath against house of *I.* is in danger to be hewn down

D&C 18:6 house of *I.* must be stirred up to repent;

D&C 42:39 the Lord to consecrate riches of Gentiles to poor of house of *I.*;

D&C 77:11 hundred forty-four thousand to be sealed out of all tribes of *I.*;

D&C 84:23 Moses taught *I.* in wilderness;

D&C 103:17 Saints are children of *I.*;

D&C 113:10 bands on Zion's neck are God's curses on *I.* in scattered condition;

D&C 133:34 blessings of God upon tribes of *I.*;

D&C 136:22 I am he who led children of *I.*;

D&C 138:25 the Savior spent three years in ministry to those of house of *I*

Moses 1:26 God calls *I.* his chosen;

Moses 1:26 *I.* to be delivered by Moses.

Israel Gathering:
1 Ne. 10:3 Jerusalem to be carried captive into Babylon;
1 Ne. 10:12 (Jacob 5:7–8 , 13–14) house of *I.* compared to olive-tree whose branches should be broken off and scattered;
1 Ne. 10:14 (15:12–18; 3 Ne. 16:4, 11–12) *I.* to be gathered again, to come to knowledge of the Messiah;
1 Ne. 10:14 (Jacob 5:52–74) natural branches of olive-tree, remnants of *I.,* to be grafted in;
1 Ne. 10:14 (15:16–17; 2 Ne. 6:11; 10:6–7; 3 Ne. 20:13) after *I.* is scattered, they will be gathered;
1 Ne. 13:14 (22:7; 3 Ne. 16:8; Morm. 5:9) seed of Lamanites to be scattered by Gentiles;
1 Ne. 15:18–20 (2 Ne. 3:21; 3 Ne. 10:7; 16:5, 20:12–13, 29; 21:4, 7; 29:1, 3, 8–9) God to remember covenant to restore *I.;*
1 Ne. 15:20 after being gathered, *I.* will be scattered no more;
1 Ne. 19:16 (3 Ne. 5:24) all people who are of house of *I.* will the Lord gather in;
1 Ne. 21:1 house of *I.* are broken off and driven out because of wickedness of pastors;
1 Ne. 21:5–6 (Isa. 49:5–6) Isaiah[1] to be servant to raise up tribes of Jacob and restore preserved of *I.;*
1 Ne. 21:22 (Isa. 49:22) Gentiles shall bring *I*'s sons and daughters;
1 Ne. 22:3, 7 (2 Ne. 25:15) house of *I.* to be scattered among all nations;
1 Ne. 22:4 many are already lost from knowledge of those at Jerusalem;
2 Ne. 3:5 from loins of Joseph[1] would come righteous branch to be broken off;
2 Ne. 3:11–13 latter-day seer to be raised up when work commences unto restoring house of *I.;*
2 Ne. 3:24 mighty one to rise up as instrument of the Lord in bringing to pass much restoration unto house of *I.;*
2 Ne. 6:14 (21:11; 25:17; 29:1; Jacob 6:2; Isa. 11:11) the Messiah will set hand second time to recover covenant people of *I.;*
2 Ne. 9:2 the Lord speaks to *I.* by prophets until time when they are restored to true Church and gathered to lands of inheritance;
2 Ne. 10:2 (30:5; Hel. 15:11; 3 Ne. 5:23) descendants of Nephites and Lamanites to be restored to knowledge of Christ;
2 Ne. 10:22 God has led away from time to time from house of *I.;*
2 Ne. 20:22 (Isa. 10:22) though *I.* be as sand of sea, yet remnant shall return;
2 Ne. 21:12 (Isa. 11:12) the Lord shall assemble outcasts of *I.;*
2 Ne. 24:2 (Isa. 14:2) house of *I.* to return to lands of promise;

2 Ne. 30:7–8 (3 Ne. 20:31–33; Morm. 5:14) Jews shall begin to believe in Christ, and God will commence work of restoration;

Omni 1:15 (Hel. 8:21) people of Zarahemla come from Jerusalem when Zedekiah was taken captive into Babylon;

3 Ne. 10:4–6 (Matt. 23:37) the Lord would gather *l.* as hen gathers chickens;

3 Ne. 10:7 place of *l's* dwellings shall be desolate until fulfilling of covenant;

3 Ne. 16:4 through fulness of Gentiles, remnant of *l.* shall be brought to knowledge of the Redeemer;

3 Ne. 20:27 Gentiles to be made mighty unto scattering of Israel;

3 Ne. 20:29 the Lord will remember covenant to gather his people and give them Jerusalem as land of inheritance;

3 Ne. 21:22–24 Gentiles shall assist remnant of Jacob in gathering unto New Jerusalem;

3 Ne. 21:27 work to commence among dispersed to prepare way, that they call upon the Father in Christ's name;

3 Ne. 28:29 Three Nephites to minister to scattered tribes of Israel;

3 Ne. 29:1 when scriptures come to Gentiles, the Father's covenant to restore *l.* to lands of inheritance will be fulfilled;

Ether 13:7 the Lord brought remnant of seed of Joseph out of Jerusalem

Morm. 3:17 when work commences, *l.* shall be about to prepare to return to land of inheritance;

Morm. 5:14 writings to convince Jews, that the Father may restore house of *l.* to land of inheritance;

Ether 4:14 come unto me, ye house of *l.*;

Ether 13:10 seed of Joseph[1] who are of house of *l.*, shall dwell in New Jerusalem.

D&C 18:6 house of *l.* must be stirred up to repent;

D&C 42:39 the Lord to consecrate riches of Gentiles to poor of house of *l.*;

D&C 84:23 Moses taught *l.* in wilderness;

D&C 103:17 Saints are children of *l.*;

D&C 133:34 blessings of God upon tribes of *l.*;

D&C 136:22 I am he who led children of *l.*;

D&C 138:25 the Savior spent three years in ministry to those of house of *l*

Moses 1:26 God calls *l.* his chosen;

Moses 1:26 *l.* to be delivered by Moses.

2 Ne. 29:12 the Lord will speak to Jews, Nephites, other tribes, and they shall write;

2 Ne. 29:13 Jews, Nephites, and lost tribes shall have each others' writings;

3 Ne. 15:15 the Father has not commanded Christ to tell Jews about other tribes whom the Father led away;

3 Ne. 15:20 the Father separated other tribes from Jews because of iniquity;

3 Ne. 17:4 Christ will show himself to lost tribes;

3 Ne. 21:26 gospel to be preached to lost tribes;

Ether 13:11 they who were scattered and gathered from north countries are partakers of fulfilling of covenant

D&C 45:19 Christ prophesied that Jews would be destroyed and scattered among all nations;

D&C 113:10 scattered remnants are exhorted to return to the Lord.

Israel Ten Lost Tribes of:

1 Ne. 5:14 Lehi[1] descendant of Joseph who was son of *J.*;

1 Ne. 6:4 (19:10; Mosiah 7:19; 23:23; Alma 29:11; 36:2; 3 Ne. 4:30; Morm. 9:11) God of Abraham, Isaac, and *J.*;

1 Ne. 17:40 the Lord covenanted with Abraham, Isaac, and *J.*;

1 Ne. 20:20 (Isa. 48:20) the Lord hath redeemed his servant *J.*;

2 Ne. 12:3 (Isa. 2:3) let us go up to house of the God of *J.*;

2 Ne. 19:8 the Lord sent his word unto *J.*, and it hath lighted upon Israel;

Alma 5:24 (7:25; Hel. 3:30) righteous shall sit down in kingdom of God with Abraham, Isaac, and *J.*;

Alma 46:24–26 remember words of *J.* before his death;

3 Ne. 10:17 father *J.* testified concerning remnant of seed of Joseph;

3 Ne. 20:22 this people will Christ establish in this land unto fulfilling of covenant made with father *J*

D&C 110:11 Moses commits keys of leading of ten tribes from north;

D&C 133:26–34 those in north countries shall come

A of F 10 we believe in restoration of ten tribes.

Jacob - father of twelve tribes

1 Ne. 20:1, 12 hear this, O house of *J.*, who are called by name of Israel;

1 Ne. 20:20 the Lord hath redeemed his servant *J.*;

1 Ne. 21:5 Isaiah to be the Lord's servant to bring tribes of *J.* again to him;

2 Ne. 12:5 (Isa. 2:5) O house of *J.*, let us walk in light of the Lord;

2 Ne. 12:6 (Isa. 2:6) O Lord, thou hast forsaken thy people, house of *J.*;

2 Ne. 19:8 the Lord sent his word unto *J.*, and it hath lighted upon Israel;

2 Ne. 20:20 such as are escaped of house of *J.* shall no more stay upon him that smote them;

2 Ne. 24:1 the Lord will have mercy on *J.* and strangers shall cleave to house of *J.*;

Alma 46:23 (3 Ne. 20:16; 21:2; Morm. 7:10) Nephites are remnant of seed of *J.*;

3 Ne. 5:24 the Lord to gather all remnant of seed of *J.*;

3 Ne. 5:25 the Lord hath covenanted with all house of *J.*;

3 Ne. 10:4 how oft would the Lord have gathered descendants of *J.*;
3 Ne. 21:22 if Gentiles repent, they will be numbered among this remnant of *J.*;
3 Ne. 21:23 Gentiles to assist remnant of *J.* in building New Jerusalem;
4 Ne. 1:49 (Morm. 5:12) sacred records to come again unto remnant of house of *J*
D&C 27:10 Joseph[1] *J.*, Isaac, Abraham, by whom promises remain;
D&C 98:32 law given unto *J.*;
D&C 132:1, 37 the Lord justified *J.* in having many wives and concubines;
D&C 133:55 *J.* shall be in presence of the Lamb;
D&C 136:21 God of Abraham, Isaac, *J.*;
D&C 138:41 Joseph F. Smith saw *J.* among noble spirits.

Jacob House of:
1 Ne. 5:13 brass plates contain prophecies of *J.*;
1 Ne. 7:14 Jews have cast *J.* into prison;
Hel. 8:20 testified of Jerusalem's destruction
D&C 10:60 the Lord's other sheep are branch of house of *J.*;
D&C 49:24 *J.* to flourish in wilderness before the Lord's coming;
D&C 52:2 the Lord's people are remnant of *J.*;
D&C 109:62 have mercy upon children of *J.*;
D&C 109:65 remnant of *J.* smitten because of transgression will be converted.

Jeremiah - Hebrew prophet:
1 Ne. 1:4, 7 Lehi[1] dwells at *J.*;
1 Ne. 1:4, 13, 18 (2:13; 3:17; 7:13; 10:3; 2 Ne. 25:14; Alma 9:9; Hel. 8:20–21.

Jerusalem:
Ether 13:5) destruction of *J.*;
Ether 2:4 (17:20; Alma 10:3; Hel. 5:6) Lehi[1] and family leave *J.*;
Ether 2:11 (2 Ne. 1:1, 3; Jacob 2:25, 32; Omni 1:6; Mosiah 2:4; 7:20; Alma 9:22; 22:9; 36:29; 3 Ne. 5:20; Ether 13:7) the Lord leads Lehites out of land of *J.*;
Ether 3:2–4:38 (5:6; 7:2) sons of Lehi return to *J.* for records;
Ether 5:4 (19:20) family of Lehi[1] would have perished if they had remained at *J.*;
Ether 7:3–5 sons of Lehi return to *J.* to get family of Ishmael;
Ether 10:4 (19:8) the Messiah to come six hundred years after Lehi left *J.*;
Ether 11:13 Nephi[1] sees *J.* in vision;
Ether 18:24 Lehites bring seeds from land of *J.*;
Ether 19:13 (4 Ne. 1:31) those at *J.* shall crucify God of Israel;
Ether 22:4 many already lost from knowledge of those at *J.*;

2 Ne. 1:4 (6:8) Lehi sees in vision that *J.* is destroyed;

2 Ne. 8:17 (Isa. 51:17) *J.* has drunk cup of the Lord's fury;

2 Ne. 9:5 God shall show himself to those at *J.*;

2 Ne. 10:5 those at *J.* shall stiffen their necks;

2 Ne. 12:1 (Isa. 2:1) word Isaiah saw concerning Judah and *J.*;

2 Ne. 13:1 (Isa. 3:1) the Lord takes away from *J.* stay and staff;

2 Ne. 14:3 (Isa. 4:3) they who remain in *J.* shall be called holy;

2 Ne. 17:1 (Isa. 7:1) kings of Syria and Israel went up toward *J.* to war against it;

2 Ne. 18:14 (Isa. 8:14) the Lord shall be for gin and snare to inhabitants of *J.*;

2 Ne. 20:32 (Isa. 10:32) the Lord shall shake hand against mount of daughter of Zion, hill of *J.*;

2 Ne. 25:6 Nephi has dwelt at *J.*;

2 Ne. 25:11 Jews will return and possess land of *J.*;

2 Ne. 30:4 remnant of Nephites' seed shall know they came from *J.*;

Jacob 2:31 the Lord has heard mourning of his people in land of *J.*;

Mosiah 1:6 records contain sayings of fathers from time they came from *J.*;

Mosiah 12:23 (15:30; 3 Ne. 16:19) the Lord has redeemed *J.*;

Alma 3:11 (10:17) brass plates brought out of land of *J.*;

Alma 7:10 the Son shall be born at *J.*;

3 Ne. 4:11 greatest slaughter among people of Lehi since he left *J.*;

3 Ne. 10:5 how oft would the Lord have gathered his people that dwell at *J.*;

3 Ne. 15:14 Christ not commanded to tell those at *J.* about Nephites;

3 Ne. 16:1 the Lord has other sheep not of this land or land of *J.*;

3 Ne. 17:8 Nephites desire that Christ show what he has done unto brethren at *J.*;

3 Ne. 20:29 land of *J.* is Israel's promised land forever;

3 Ne. 20:46 *J.* shall be inhabited again.

Morm. 3:18 twelve tribes of Israel shall be judged by twelve disciples in land of *J.*;

Ether 13:8 remnant of house of Joseph shall build holy city, like *J.* of old;

Ether 13:11 then cometh *J.* of old;

Moro. 10:31 awake and arise from dust, O *J.*

2 Ne. 21:1 (Isa. 11:1) there shall come forth rod out of stem of *J.*;

2 Ne. 21:10 (Isa. 11:10) there shall be root of *J.*, which shall stand for ensign

D&C 45:18–25 Christ's prediction concerning *J.*;

D&C 77:15 Jews to gather and build city of *J.*;

D&C 109:62 *J.* to be redeemed;

D&C 124:36 baptisms for dead in *J.*;

D&C 133:24 land of *J.* to be turned back into its own place

JS—M 1:12, 18, 21 tribulation and destruction to come upon *J.* in latter days.

Jesse:

Morm. 3:21 Jews to have other witnesses that Jesus, whom they slew, was the very Christ

D&C 113:1–6 stem of *J.*

Jesus Christ:

1 Ne. 10:11 after the Messiah has been slain by Jews, he shall rise from dead;

1 Ne. 11:33 (Alma 30:26; 3 Ne. 11:14) the Son to be lifted up upon cross and slain for sins of world;

1 Ne. 19:10 (Hel. 14:14, 20, 27; 3 Ne. 8:3, 19–23; 10:9) three days of darkness to be sign of Christ's death;

1 Ne. 19:13 (2 Ne. 10:3, 5; 25:13; Morm. 3:21) Jews to crucify God;

2 Ne. 2:8 the Messiah lays down life according to flesh;

2 Ne. 6:9 (Mosiah 3:9) Jews will scourge and crucify the Holy One, Jesus Christ;

2 Ne. 9:5 the great Creator suffers himself to die for all men;

2 Ne. 10:3 no other nation would crucify their God;

2 Ne. 26:3 signs to be given of the Messiah's birth, death, resurrection

D&C 45:52 Jesus will proclaim himself to Jews;

D&C 50:41 Christ has overcome world;

D&C 59:5 serve God in name of Jesus Christ;

D&C 60:4 Christ rules in heavens above;

D&C 62:1 Jesus Christ knows men's weaknesses and how to succor them;

D&C 62:6 he cannot lie;

D&C 68:6 elders to bear record of Jesus Christ;

D&C 76:13 (93:21) premortal existence of Jesus Christ

D&C 113:1–2 (Isa. 11:1–5) the Stem of Jesse;

D&C 132:24 to have eternal lives is to know God and Jesus Christ

Moses 6:52, 57 (7:50) name of the Only Begotten is the Son of Man, even Jesus Christ;

JS—H 1:40 prophet mentioned in Acts 3:22–23 is Christ;

A of F 1 we believe in God, the Eternal Father, and in His Son, Jesus Christ;

A of F 10 we believe that Christ will reign personally upon earth.

Jesus Christ Death of:

1 Ne. 19:14 (22:5; 2 Ne. 6:10) because Jews have despised the Holy One, they shall wander in flesh;

1 Ne. 20:17 (21:7) the Lord, thy Redeemer, the Holy One;

1 Ne. 22:18 (2 Ne. 1:10; 6:10, 15; 15:24) wrath to be poured out on those who harden hearts against the Holy One;
1 Ne. 22:21 prophet of whom Moses spoke was the Holy One;
1 Ne. 22:28 all who repent will dwell safely in the Holy One;
2 Ne. 2:10 ends of law which the Holy One hath given;
2 Ne. 3:2 land to be consecrated unto those who keep commandments of the Holy One;
2 Ne. 6:9 the Holy One to manifest himself to Jews in flesh;
2 Ne. 9:11–12 temporal death to deliver its dead through power of Resurrection of the Holy One;
2 Ne. 9:15 (Morm. 9:13–14) those resurrected must appear before judgment-seat of the Holy One;
2 Ne. 9:18 those who have believed in the Holy One shall inherit kingdom of God;
2 Ne. 9:19 the Holy One delivers his Saints from death and Hell;
2 Ne. 9:23 men must be baptized having faith in the Holy One;
2 Ne. 9:25 mercies of the Holy One have claim because of Atonement;
2 Ne. 9:26 all to be restored to the God who gave them breath, the Holy One;
2 Ne. 9:41 keeper of gate is the Holy One;
2 Ne. 25:29 (30:2; Omni 1:26) Christ is the Holy One of Israel;
2 Ne. 27:34 children of Jacob shall sanctify the Holy One;
3 Ne. 22:5 (Isa. 54:5) thy maker, thy Redeemer, the Holy One
Moses 7:47 the Righteous is lifted up;

Jesus Christ—Holy One of Israel:
2 Ne. 11:4 (Jacob 4:5; Mosiah 13:30–31; 16:14; Alma 25:15; 34:14; Gal. 3:24; Heb. 10:1) law of Moses given as type pointing to Christ;
2 Ne. 11:4 all things given of God from beginning typify Christ;
Jacob 4:5 Avraham's offering up of Isaac is similitude of God and the Son;
Mosiah 3:15 the Lord showed his people many types of his coming;
Alma 33:19–21 (1 Ne. 17:41; 2 Ne. 25:20; Hel. 8:14–15; Num. 21:8–9) serpent raised in wilderness a type of Christ.

Jesus Christ: Messiah:
D&C 13:1 priesthood conferred in name of Messiah;
D&C 19:27 Jews to stop looking for a Messiah to come who has come;
D&C 109:67 scattered remnants of Israel to believe in the Messiah
Moses 7:53 blessed is he through whose seed Messiah shall come;
Moses 7:53 the Lord saith, I am Messiah, King of Zion;
JS—H 1:69 priesthood conferred in name of Messiah.

Jesus Christ Types of:

Title Page (2 Ne. 26:12) book written to convincing of *J.* and Gentile that Jesus is the Christ;

1 Ne. 1:2 language of Lehi consists of learning of *J.* and language of Egyptians;

1 Ne. 1:19–20 *J.* mock Lehi;

1 Ne. 2:13 (17:44) *J.* seek to kill Lehi;

1 Ne. 3:3 (5:6) Laban has record of *J.*;

1 Ne. 5:12 (Omni 1:14; Ether 1:3) brass plates contain record of *J.* down to Zedekiah;

1 Ne. 10:4 the Lord will raise up a Messiah among *J.*;

1 Ne. 10:11 *J.* to hear gospel, dwindle in unbelief;

1 Ne. 13:23–24, 38 (14:23; 2 Ne. 29:4–13) book containing record of *J.*, covenants of the Lord to come from *J.*;

1 Ne. 13:25–26 (Morm. 7:8) gospel goes forth in purity from *J.* to Gentiles;

1 Ne. 13:39 (2 Ne. 25:15; 30:7) *J.* to be scattered;

1 Ne. 13:42 the Lamb shall be manifest to *J.*, then Gentiles, to Gentiles, then *J.*;

1 Ne. 15:17 (2 Ne. 25:18) the Lord will be rejected of *J.*;

1 Ne. 15:19–20 Nephi rehearses words of Isaiah concerning restoration of *J.*;

2 Ne. 9:2 the Lord has spoken unto *J.* by mouth of prophets;

2 Ne. 10:3 (4 Ne. 1:31; Morm. 7:5) Christ to come among *J.*, for no other nation would crucify their God;

2 Ne. 25:1, 5–6 difficulty of understanding manner of prophesying among *J.*;

2 Ne. 25:9 *J.* have been destroyed from generation to generation according to iniquities;

2 Ne. 26:33 all are alike unto God, both Gentile and *J.*;

2 Ne. 27:1 in last days all nations of Gentiles and *J.* shall be drunken with iniquity;

2 Ne. 30:2 *J.* who will not repent shall be cast off;

2 Ne. 30:4 remnant of Nephites' seed shall know they are descendants of *J.*;

2 Ne. 33:8 Nephi has charity for *J.*, whence he came;

2 Ne. 33:10 Nephi admonishes *J.* to believe in Christ;

2 Ne. 33:14 words of *J.* will condemn those who do not accept them;

Jacob 4:14 *J.* stiffnecked people;

Jacob 4:15–17 by stumbling of *J.*, they will reject stone upon which they might build safe foundation;

Alma 11:4 Nephites do not reckon after manner of *J.*;

Alma 16:13 synagogues built after manner of *J.*;

3 Ne. 19:35 so great faith have 1 Never seen among all *J.*;

3 Ne. 28:28 Three Nephites will be among *J.*;
3 Ne. 29:8 Gentiles need no longer spurn or make game of *J.*;
Morm. 3:21 *J.* shall have other witnesses that Jesus, whom they slew, is the Christ;
Morm. 5:12, 14 writings shall go unto unbelieving of *J.*

Joseph:
1 Ne. 1:4 (5:12; Omni 1:15) Zedekiah, king of *J.*;
1 Ne. 20:1 (Isa. 48:1) house of Jacob are come forth out of waters of *J.*, or waters of baptism;
2 Ne. 3:12 fruit of loins of *J.* shall write;
2 Ne. 12:1 (Isa. 2:1) word that Isaiah saw concerning *J.* and Jerusalem;
2 Ne. 13:8 (Isa. 3:8) *J.* is fallen;
2 Ne. 17:6 (Isa. 7:6) let us go up against *J.* and vex it;
2 Ne. 17:17 (Isa. 7:17) day that Ephraim departed from *J.*;
2 Ne. 21:13 (Isa. 11:13) Ephraim shall not envy *J.*, and *J.* shall not vex Ephraim
2 Ne. 3:16 (25:21) the Lord promised *J.* to preserve his seed forever;
Jacob 2:25 Nephites to be righteous branch from loins of *J.*;
Alma 46:23 (Ether 13:7) Nephites are remnant of seed of *J.*;
Alma 46:24–27 (3 Ne. 10:17) part of remnant of *J.* shall be preserved, as remnant of coat of *J.*, remainder shall perish;
3 Ne. 15:12 Nephites remnant of house of *J.*;
Ether 13:6–10 New Jerusalem to be built unto remnant of seed of *J.*
D&C 90:10 house of *J.* to be convinced of gospel;
D&C 113:6 root of Jesse to be descendant of *J.*

Language
1 Ne. 1:2 (Mosiah 1:4) Nephi writes in *l.* of father, which consists of learning of Jews and *l.* of Egyptians.

Law of Moses
1 Ne. 4:16 *l.* was engraven upon brass plates;
1 Ne. 17:22 people of Jerusalem were righteous, kept commandments according to *l.* of Moses;
2 Ne. 5:10 (25:24; Jarom 1:5; Alma 30:3) Nephites kept commandments according to *l.* of Moses;
2 Ne. 11:4 (25:24–30; Jacob 4:5–6; Alma 25:15; 34:14) *l.* of Moses has been given to point people toward Christ;
2 Ne. 25:25 *l.* is dead unto us, and we are alive in Christ;
2 Ne. 25:25 we keep *l.* because of commandments;
Mosiah 3:14 because his people were stiffnecked, the Lord gave them *l.* of Moses;
Mosiah 12:28–29 if ye teach *l.* of Moses, why do ye not keep it;

Mosiah 13:30–32 *l.* of performances and ordinances given to keep people in remembrance of God;

3 Ne. 1:24–25 some teach that Nephites should not observe *l.* of Moses because Christ has been born;

3 Ne. 9:17 (12:17–18; 15:4–5; Matt. 5:17–18) in Christ is *l.* of Moses fulfilled;

3 Ne. 12:17 (Matt. 5:17) think not that I am come to destroy *l.*;

3 Ne. 12:18 (Matt. 5:18) not one jot nor one tittle hath passed away from *l*

D&C 22:2 men cannot enter strait gate by *l.* of Moses;

D&C 74:3 unbelieving husband wanted children circumcised and subject to *l.* of Moses;

D&C 84:27 preparatory gospel is *l.* of carnal commandments

D&C 22:2 men cannot enter strait gate by *l.* of Moses;

D&C 74:3 unbelieving husband wanted children circumcised and subject to *l.* of Moses;

D&C 84:27 preparatory gospel is *l.* of carnal commandments.

Lehi - Hebrew prophet

1 Ne. 1:5 prays to the Lord on behalf of his people;

1 Ne. 1:6–15 sees visions;

1 Ne. 1:16 writes many things he has seen in visions and dreams;

1 Ne. 1:18–20 (Hel. 8:22) prophesies among Jews, is rejected;

1 Ne. 2:1–4 (Alma 9:9; 10:3; Hel. 8:22; Ether 13:5) flees Jerusalem with family;

1 Ne. 3:2–4 sends sons to obtain brass plates;

1 Ne. 5:10–15 (Mosiah 1:4) reads brass plates;

1 Ne. 5:14 (2 Ne. 3:4; Alma 10:3) descendant of Joseph;

1 Ne. 5:17–19 prophesies concerning his seed and brass plates;

1 Ne. 10:2–16 prophesies Babylonian captivity, coming of Christ, future of Jews.

Look

1 Ne. 17:40–41 (Alma 33:19–20; Hel. 8:14–15) labor which Israelites had to perform to be healed was to *l.* upon serpent;

2 Ne. 2:28 *l.* to the great Mediator;

2 Ne. 8:1 (Isa. 51:1) *l.* unto rock from whence ye are hewn;

2 Ne. 24:16 (Isa. 14:16) they that see thee shall narrowly *l.* upon thee;

2 Ne. 25:24 (26:8) *l.* forward unto Christ;

2 Ne. 25:27 by knowing deadness of law, they may *l.* forward unto that life which is in Christ;

Jacob 4:14 Jews' blindness came by *l.* beyond mark

D&C 19:27 Jews to believe gospel and *l.* not for the Messiah to come who has already come;

D&C 45:43–44 remnant shall *l.* for the Lord;

D&C 45:51 Jews shall *l.* upon the Savior.

Lose Lost
3 Ne. 17:4 go ... to show myself unto the *l.* tribes of Israel
3 Ne. 21:26 work of the Father commence among tribes which have been
    l.

Moses
1 Ne. 4:2 let us be strong like unto *M.*;
1 Ne. 17:24–26 (2 Ne. 3:10) *M.* is commanded to lead Israel out of
    bondage;
1 Ne. 17:24 *M.* smote rock, water came forth;
1 Ne. 17:30, 42 Israelites reviled against *M.*;
1 Ne. 22:20–21 (3 Ne. 20:23; 21:11; Deut. 18:15) Christ is prophet like
    unto *M.* that the Lord would raise;
2 Ne. 3:9–17 latter-day prophet like unto *M.* to be named Joseph;
2 Ne. 25:20 (Hel. 8:11–13) *M.* was given power by God;
Mosiah 12:33 the Lord delivered commandments to *M.* in mount of Sinai;
Mosiah 13:5 Abinadi's face shines even as *M.*;
Mosiah 13:33 *M.* prophesied about the Messiah;
D&C 8:3 *M.* led Israel by revelation;
D&C 28:2 Joseph Smith received commandments as did *M.*;
D&C 84:6 *M.* received priesthood from Jethro;
D&C 84:23–26 why *M.* was taken away from Israel;
D&C 84:31–32 sons of *M.* and Aaron shall offer acceptable offering, be
    filled with glory in the Lord's house;
D&C 84:33–34 those who magnify priesthood calling become sons of *M.*
    and Aaron;
D&C 103:16–18 man like *M.* promised;
D&C 110:11 *M.* commits keys of gathering Israel;
D&C 124:38 tabernacle built by *M.* for sacred ordinances;
D&C 133:63 prediction of *M.* to be fulfilled;
D&C 138:41 *M.* the great law–giver of Israel is seen among noble spirits;
D&C 138:45 *M.* appeared with Elias on Mount of Transfiguration
Moses 1:1 *M.* is caught up into mountain;
Moses 1:2, 31 sees God face to face;
Moses 1:2, 11, 31 glory of God is upon *M.*;
Moses 1:4 is called son of God;
Moses 1:6, 13 *M.* is in similitude of the Only Begotten;
Moses 1:8, 27–29 *M.* beholds world and its inhabitants;
Moses 1:9 presence of God is withdrawn from *M.*;
Moses 1:10 *M.* knows that man is nothing;
Moses 1:11 *M.* is transfigured before God;
Moses 1:12 Satan tempts *M.*;

Moses 1:12, 19 Satan commands *M.* to worship him;
Moses 1:13 *M.* affirms himself a son of God;
Moses 1:14, 20–21 *M.* receives strength from God;
Moses 1:15, 18 *M.* can judge between Satan and God;
Moses 1:26 *M.* is to deliver Israel from bondage;

Nature Natural
1 Ne. 10:14 (15:7) *n.* branches of olive tree are remnant of house of Israel;
1 Ne. 19:12 the God of *n.* suffers;
Jacob 5:3–77 parable of olive tree, with *n.* branches and fruit.

North
3 Ne. 20:13 scattered remnant shall be gathered from east, west, south, *n*
D&C 110:11 (133:26) ten tribes to come from *n.* country;

Obscurity
1 Ne. 22:12 Israel shall be brought out of *o.*

Observe
Mosiah 13:30 Israelites given law of performances to *o.*;
Mosiah 18:23 Alma commands his people to *o.* Sabbath day.

Ordinance
2 Ne. 25:30 keep performances and *o.* until law is fulfulled;
Mosiah 13:30 children of Israel given law of performances and *o.* to keep them in remembrance of God;
Alma 13:8 high priests ordained with holy *o.*
Alma 13:16 *o.* given that people might look forward on the Son;
Alma 30:3 Nephites are strict in observing *o.* according to law of Moses
D&C 1:15 men have strayed from the Lord's *o.*;
D&C 52:15–16 the Lord accepts those who obey his *o.*;
D&C 64:5 Joseph Smith given keys of mysteries if he obeys *o.*;
D&C 77:14 (Rev. 10:2, 9–10) John's little book was mission and *o.* to gather Israel;
D&C 84:20–21 in *o.* of Melchizedek Priesthood is power of godliness manifest;
D&C 88:139–40 *o.* of washing of feet instituted to receive men into School of Prophets;
D&C 107:14, 20 Aaronic Priesthood to administer outward *o.*;
D&C 124:33 build house wherein *o.* of baptizing for dead belongs;
D&C 128:8 nature of *o.* of baptism for dead consists in binding power of priesthood;
D&C 138:54 great latter-day work to include temple *o.*;

Peace
2 Ne. 3:12 writings of Nephites and Jews shall grow together unto establishing *p.*;

People
2 Ne. 29:4–5 Jews, the Lord's ancient covenant *p.*;
2 Ne. 29:14 the Lord's *p.*, who are of house of Israel, shall be gathered.

Perish
1 Ne. 5:19 brass plates should never *p.*;
1 Ne. 15:10 how is it ye will *p.* because of hardness of heart;
2 Ne. 1:4 if Lehites had stayed in Jerusalem, they would have *p.*;
2 Ne. 6:11 many Jews shall be afflicted in flesh and not suffered to *p.* because of prayers of righteous;

Plates Brass
1 Ne. 3:3, 12 (19:2) Laban has record of Jews and genealogy of fathers engraven on *b. p.*;
1 Ne. 3:9–4:38 sons of Lehi obtain *b. p.*;
1 Ne. 4:16 law is engraven upon *b. p.*;
1 Ne. 4:24 Nephi to carry engravings on *b. p.* to brothers;
1 Ne. 5:10–16 (19:23; Omni 1:14; Alma 37:3) *b. p.* contain five books of Moses, history of Jews to reign of Zedekiah, genealogy;
1 Ne. 5:18 *b. p.* to go to every people of seed of Lehi;
1 Ne. 5:19 *b. p.* should never perish;
1 Ne. 7:11 ye have forgotten what great things the Lord hath done that we should obtain record;
1 Ne. 13:23 Bible is like engravings on *b. p.*

Preserve
1 Ne. 3:19–20 sons of Lehi should obtain brass plates to *p.* language and words of prophets;
1 Ne. 5:21 brass plates of great value in *p.* commandments;
2 Ne. 3:16 the Lord covenants to *p.* seed of Joseph[1] forever
Abr. 1:31 the Lord *p.* fathers' records in Avraham's hands.

Priesthood Melchizedek
Alma 4:20 Alma confines himself wholly to high *p.* of holy order of God;
Alma 13:1–12 men are ordained unto high *p.* of holy order of God, after order of the Son;
Alma 13:7–9 high *p.* after order of the Son was from foundation of world, without beginning of days or end of years;
Alma 13:14, 18 Melchizedek took upon himself high p. forever
D&C 76:57 order of M. P. is after order of Enoch, order of the Son;

D&C 84:17 M. P. continues in Church of God in all generations;

D&C 81:2 keys belong to Presidency of High P.;

D&C 84:6–7 (107:40–41) lineage of Holy P. from Adam to Moses;

D&C 84:18 Aaronic P. abides forever with p. after holiest order of God;

D&C 84:20–21 only in ordinances of M. P. is power of godliness manifest;

D&C 107:3 (124:123) before Melchizedek it was called Holy P. after Order of the Son of God;

D&C 107:5 all authorities and offices of Church are appendages to this p.;

D&C 107:8–10 M. P. holds right of presidency, administers in spiritual things;

D&C 107:18 M. P. holds keys of all spiritual blessings of Church;

D&C 107:65–66 one to be appointed of High P. to preside over p.;

D&C 124:123 officers of p. hold keys of M. P.;

D&C 131:2 in order to enter highest degree of celestial kingdom, man must enter into *p.* order of marriage;

D&C 132:7 only one on earth at a time to whom sealing power and keys of *p.* are given;

D&C 132:45 I have conferred upon you keys and power of *p*

JS—H 1:72 Peter, James, and John hold keys of *M. P.*

Promised Land

1Ne. 17:38 the Lord leads away righteous into precious lands;

1Ne. 22:12 (**2** Ne. 6:11; 9:2; 10:7; 25:11; 3 Ne. 20:33; 29:1) Israel to be gathered to land of inheritance;

2 Ne. 9:2 Jews shall be established in all their lands of *p.*;

2 Ne. 24:2 (Isa. 14:2) Israel shall return to lands of *p.*;

Jacob 2:12 land of *p.* abounds in precious metals;

Enos 1:10 I have given thy brethren this holy land;

3 Ne. 20:29 the Father will remember covenant to give his people again land of Jerusalem, which is *p. l.* , unto them forever;

3 Ne. 21:22 the Lord has given land to remnant of Jacob for their inheritance

D&C 77:15 two prophets to be raised up after Jews have built Jerusalem in land of fathers;

D&C 103:11 scattered brethren shall return to lands of inheritances and build waste places of Zion;

D&C 124:38 Israel was commanded to build house for ordinances in land of *p*

Abr. 2:19 unto thy seed will I give this land.

Prophecy Prophesy

2 Ne. 25:1 words of Isaiah are hard for Nephites to understand because they know not Jew's manner of *p.*;

2 Ne. 25:4 words of Isaiah are plain to all who are filled with spirit of *p.*

Prophet:
1 Ne. 3:18 (7:14; 2 Ne. 27:5) Jews have rejected words of *p.*;
1 Ne. 10:4 six hundred years after Lehi left Jerusalem, the Lord would raise up *p.*, a Messiah;
1 Ne. 11:27 *p.* should prepare way before the Redeemer;
1 Ne. 19:20 had not the Lord shown Nephi concerning Jews, as he had *p.* of old, he should have perished;
1 Ne. 22:2 by the Spirit are all things made known unto *p.*;
1 Ne. 22:20–21 (3 Ne. 20:23) the Lord will raise up *p.* like unto Moses, the Holy One;
2 Ne. 25:5 Jews understand words of *p.*;
1 Ne. 25:18 only one Messiah spoken of by *p.*;
1 Ne. 26:3 (Jacob 4:14) Jews shall perish because they killed *p*
Jacob 7:15 two *p.* to be raised up to Jewish nation;
D&C 84:2 Church established as predicted by *p.*;
D&C 98:17 hearts of Jews to be turned to *p.*;
D&C 127:4 (136:36) they persecuted *p.* before you;
D&C 133:26 *p.* of lost tribes shall hear the Lord's voice;
D&C 138:32 gospel taught to those who rejected *p.*;
D&C 138:36 spirits of *p.* are prepared to carry gospel to dead spirits

Purity Pure
1 Ne. 13:25 gospel goes forth in *p.* from Jews to Gentiles;
1 Ne. 14:26 sealed writings shall come forth in *p.*;
2 Ne. 9:14 righteous shall have perfect knowledge of their righteousness, being clothed in *p.*;
2 Ne. 25:16 when Jews worship the Father with *p.* hearts and clean hands, they will believe in Christ.

Raise
1 Ne. 10:4 the Lord will *r.* the Messiah among Jews;
1 Ne. 17:37 the Lord *r.* up a righteous nation and destroys wicked nations;
1 Ne. 22:7 the Lord will *r.* up mighty nation among Gentiles;
2 Ne. 3:5 from descendants of Joseph the Lord would *r.* righteous branch of Israel;
2 Ne. 3:7 the Lord will *r.* choice seer from descendants of Joseph;
Jacob 2:30 if the Lord will *r.* seed unto himself, he will command his people

Record
1 Ne. 1:1 Nephi makes *r.* of his proceedings;
1 Ne. 1:17 Nephi abridges *r.* of father;
1 Ne. 3:3 Laban has *r.* of Jews;

1 Ne. 3:19 Lehites should obtain *r.* to preserve language of fathers;
1 Ne. 5:12 brass plates contain *r.* of Jews from beginning to reign of Zedekiah;
1 Ne. 5:16 Laban and fathers had kept *r.* because they were descendants of Joseph;
1 Ne. 6:1 *r.* of Lehi gives genealogy;
1 Ne. 10:10 John the Baptist will bear *r.* that he baptized the Lamb;
1 Ne. 11:7 Nephi to bear *r.* of the Son;
1 Ne. 12:18 the Holy Ghost bears *r.* of the Messiah;
1 Ne. 13:23 Nephi beholds book that is *r.* of Jews
Moses 1:23 *r.* of Moses lost because of men's wickedness;
Moses 1:24 (5:9; 7:11) the Holy Ghost bears *r.* of the Father and the Son;
Moses 6:63 all things made to bear *r.* of God;
Abr. 1:28 *r.* come into Abraham's hands;
Abr. 1:31 *r.* preserved in Abraham's hands.

Reject
1 Ne. 3:18 Jews have *r.* words of prophets;
1 Ne. 15:17 the Lord will show his power unto Gentiles because Jews will *r.* him;
1 Ne. 19:13 Jews shall be scourged because they *r.* signs and power of God;
2 Ne. 1:10 when those upon promised land *r.* the Holy One, judgments shall rest upon them;
2 Ne. 25:12 Jews will *r.* Christ because of iniquities;
2 Ne. 25:18 word given to Israel to convince them of the true Messiah, whom they *r.*;
2 Ne. 27:14 wo unto him who *r.* word of God;
Jacob 4:15–17 by stumbling of Jews they will *r.* stone upon which they might build safe foundation.

Remnant
1 Ne. 10:14 (15:12–13) natural branches of olive-tree, or *r.* of Israel, shall be grafted in;
1 Ne. 13:34 the Lord will visit *r.* of Israel, seed of Lehi;
2 Ne. 20:21 (Isa. 10:21) *r.* of Jacob shall return unto God;
2 Ne. 28:2 (Alma 46:23; 3 Ne. 20:16; Morm. 7:10) Nephites' seed is *r.* of house of Israel, or Jacob;
2 Ne. 30:3 Gentiles shall carry words of book to *r.* of Nephites' seed;
Alma 46:23 (**3 Ne.** 10:17; 15:12) Nephites are *r.* of seed of Joseph;
3 Ne. 5:24 the Lord will gather all *r.* of seed of Jacob;
3 Ne. 21:12 the Lord's people who are *r.* of Jacob' shall be among Gentiles;
D&C 19:27 Lamanites are *r.* of Jews;

D&C 45:24 *r.* of Jews shall scatter among nations;
D&C 45:43 *r.* shall be gathered;
D&C 52:2 the Lord's people are *r.* of Jacob;
D&C 87:5 *r.* left in land shall vex Gentiles;
D&C 109:65 *r.* of Jacob who have been cursed because of transgression will be converted;
D&C 113:10 scattered *r.* are exhorted to return
Moses 7:52 *r.* of Abraham's seed always to be found among nations of earth.

Restoration

1 Ne. 15:19 Nephi speaks concerning *r.* of Jews in latter days;
1 Ne. 21:6 (Isa. 49:6) it is light thing that thou shouldst be servant to *r.* preserved of Israel;
2 Ne. 3:24 mighty one shall rise up to do much good unto bringing to pass *r.* unto Israel;
2 Ne. 9:2 the Lord has spoken unto Jews by prophets, from beginning until they are *r.* to true Church;
2 Ne. 25:17 the Lord will set his hand second time to *r.* his people;
2 Ne. 30:8 the Lord will commence work among all nations to bring about *r.* of his people;
Jacob 7:23 peace and love of God is *r.* again among Nephites;
Alma 11:44 (40:23; 41:4) every thing shall be *r.* to its perfect frame;
Alma 40:21–22 Resurrection brings about *r.* of those things spoken by prophets;
Alma 41:2 plan of *r.* is requisite with justice of God;
D&C 27:6 (77:9, 14; 86:10) Elias given keys of *r.* all things;
D&C 45:17 the Lord to show disciples *r.* of scattered Israel;
D&C 86:10 priesthood will remain until *r.* of all things
A of F 10 we believe in *r.* of ten tribes.

Seed

3 Ne. 20:25) the Lord covenants with Abraham, In thy *s.* shall all earth be blessed;
D&C 18:24 (2 Ne. 5:11; Mosiah 9:9) Lehites plant *s.*;
2 Ne. 20:19 (Isa. 48:19) thy *s.* also had been as sand;
2 Ne. 3:3 *s.* of Joseph shall not utterly be destroyed;
2 Ne. 10:19 the Lord to consecrate this land to *s.* of Lehi;
2 Ne. 24:20 (Isa. 14:20) *s.* of evil–doers shall never be renowned;
2 Ne. 29:14 the Lord covenanted to remember Abraham's *s.* forever
D&C 84:18 (107:13) priesthood confirmed upon Aaron and his *s.*;
D&C 103:17 Saints are children of Israel and of *s.* of Abraham;
D&C 104:33 the Lord will multiply blessings upon faithful and their *s.*;
D&C 110:12 in our *s.* all generations are blessed;

D&C 124:58 (132:30) in Abraham's *s.* shall earth be blessed;
D&C 132:19 exalted shall have continuation of *s.* forever
Moses 7:52 *s.* of Noah always to be found among all nations;
Abr. 3:14 the Lord to multiply Abraham's *s.*

Serpent
2 Ne. 25:20 if Israelites would cast eyes unto *s.* raised by Moses in wilderness, they would be healed;
Hel. 8:14–15 (Alma 33:19–22) brazen *s.* lifted up by Moses in wilderness is type of Christ.

Son
1 Ne. 21:22 (22:6; 2 Ne. 6:6; Isa. 49:22) Gentiles will bring Israel's *s.* in their arms;
Jacob 4:5 Abraham's offering up his *s.,* Isaac, was similitude of God and his *S*
D&C 68:16 firstborn among *s.* of Aaron have right to bishopric;
D&C 68:21 (107:40) right of priesthood descends from father to *s*
D&C 84:30 priesthood was confirmed upon Aaron and his *s.;*
D&C 101:4 (132:36, 50) Avraham was commanded to offer his only *s.;*
D&C 128:23 all *s.* of God shouted for joy;
D&C 128:24 Lord shall purify *s.* of Levi
Abr. 1:17 God calls Avraham his *s.;*

Stone
2 Ne. 26:3 Jews *s.* prophets;
Jacob 4:15 Jews will reject *s.* upon which they might build safe foundation.

Sure Surety
1 Ne. 5:8 Sariah knows of *s.* that the Lord commanded Lehi to flee;
2 Ne. 25:7 men shall know of *s.* when prophecies of Isaiah come to pass;
Jacob 4:15–17 (Hel. 5:12) stone rejected by Jews shall be only *s.* foundation;
Mosiah 1:6 we can know of *s.* of plates because we have seen them.

Tongue
2 Ne. 13:8 Jerusalem is ruined ... because their *t.* and their doings have been against the Lord.

Tribe
1 Ne. 21:6 to raise up the *t.* of Jacob
1 Ne. 22:4 more part of all the *t.* have been led away
2 Ne. 29:12 I shall also speak unto the other *t.*
3 Ne. 7:3 every *t.* did appoint a chief

3 Ne. 15:15 (16:4; 17:4) Neither hath the Father given me commandment that I should tell unto them concerning the other *t*.
3 Ne. 28:29 shall minister unto all the scattered *t*
Morm. 3:18 I write ... unto you, twelve *t*
D&C 77:11 sealing the one hundred and forty-four thousand, out of all the *t*
D&C 110:11 keys of ... leading of the ten *t*. from the land of the north
D&C 133:34 blessing of the everlasting God upon the *t*
A of F 10 We believe in the restoration of the Ten *T*.

Twelve
1 Ne. 12:9 *t*. apostles ... shall judge the *t*. tribes
1 Ne. 14:20 one of the *t*. apostles of the Lamb
3 Ne. 12:1 (13:25) heed unto the words of these *t*
Morm. 3:18 I write ... unto you, *t*. tribes
Morm. 3:19 *t*. whom Jesus chose in this land they shall be judged by the other *t*.

Type Typify
2 Ne. 11:4 this end hath the law of Moses ... the *typifying* of him
Mosiah 3:15 *t*., and shadows showed he unto them
Mosiah 13:10 (13:31) *t*. and a shadow of things which are to come
Alma 25:15 law of Moses was a *t*. of his coming

Unbelief Unbelievers
3 Ne. 16:4 remnant ... scattered ... because of their *u*

Urim and Thummim
Mosiah 8:13 things are called interpreters
Mosiah 28:20 records, and also the interpreters
Alma 37:24 interpreters were prepared that the word of God might be fulfilled
Ether 3:23 two stones will I give unto thee
Ether 4:5 sealed up the interpreters
D&C secs. 3, 6, 11, 14 revelations given through U. and T.;
D&C 10:1 Joseph Smith given power to translate by means of U. and T.;
D&C 17:1 Three Witnesses to see U. and T. given to brother of Jared;
D&C 130:8 God's residence is great U. and T.;
D&C 130:9 earth will be U. and T.;
D&C 130:10 white stone given those who enter celestial kingdom will become U. and T.
Abr. 3:1, 4 given to Avraham;
JS—H 1:35 deposited with ancient plates;
JS—H 1:35 possession and use of stones constituted seers in ancient times;

JS—H 1:42 Joseph Smith commanded not to show U. and T. to anyone;
JS—H 1:52 first seen by Joseph Smith;
JS—H 1:59 delivered into custody of Joseph Smith.

Visit
1 Ne. 19:11 God surely shall *v.* all the house of Israel
Abr. 1:17 the Lord *v.* and destroys him who lifts hand against Abraham.

Cultural and Religious Practices

Washings/Baptism: Clarification of Rituals

As used in the Old Testament, the word *bapto*, a primary verb, means *to overwhelm, to cover with a fluid. (Strong's Exhaustive Concordance of the Bible, 1996).* In all cases, baptism refers to a single occasion. It may or may not include presenting the gift of the Holy Ghost or assuming the entrance of a holy presence into the person being baptized.

Ancient Judaism often practiced a form of what Christianity calls baptism, as noted above, in a special sense. They used Hebrew words that had somewhat different meanings than the Greek word.

Purification. In *Torah* and *Talmud*, the laws of purification are many, each with its own Hebrew root. The basic root covering all purification rituals is **Toharot** (purities). The Hebrew people practiced these rites because of a command of *Torah* that includes a set of purification laws for women, priests, converts to Judaism, and general purification for spiritual cleansing. Spiritual cleansings were also associated with physical cleansings and atonement for sin or for the desire to have oneness with God, and ONLY with God.

Levite priests, before making ritual sacrifice, used the lavers or fonts in the east court of Solomon's temple to wash themselves before each step in offering animal sacrifice on the yearly Day of Atonement, *Yom Kippur.* Various forms of washing of the outward body to symbolize inner, spiritual cleansing were common (*tavilah*=immersion). A purpose for the cleansing act is for the purpose of communing with God and becoming closer to Him, expressing thanks, love and gratitude.

It is true that no references to baptism appear in *Torah*, but it is common knowledge among Orthodox Jews through their *Torah* laws and commentaries that Jews did ritual washings in seas and in fonts to come before God as faithful followers of the Law of Moses. The Joseph Smith Translation of the Bible notes that there were baptisms from Adam's time to that of Enoch, but that it had ceased among the apostate people of Avraham's time. These **so-called baptisms were actually spiritual cleansings**—they may or may not have included immersion—to call the righteous to the study of and reverence for the canon of the Law of Moses and for repentance of various sins. There is no record or indication through Hebrew scripture that there was a baptism by immersion with regard to a Messiah in the modern sense, though they preached of a coming Messiah. In the Book of Mormon there *were* baptisms for repentance upon conversion before the Christ visited the Nephites (3 NE. 7:21-25).

We must remember that much of the Bible was edited, some was lost, and the Sanhedrin and various other groups took out scripture and changed many of the scriptures that finally were included.

Care of Dead, Mourning Practices

Jewish practices relating to death and mourning have two purposes: to show respect for the dead (*kavod ha-met*), and to comfort the living (*nihum avelim*), who will miss the deceased. Most communities have an organization to care for the dead, known as the *chevra kaddisha* (the holy society). Their volunteer work is considered extremely meritorious, because they are performing a service for someone who can never repay them.

Care of the dead. After a person dies, the eyes are closed, the body is laid on the floor and covered, and candles are lit next to the dead. The body is never left alone until after burial, as a sign of respect. The people who sit with the dead body are called *shomerim* meaning "guards". Respect for the dead body is a matter of paramount importance. *Shomerim* may not eat, drink, or perform a commandment in the presence of the dead. To do so would be considered mocking the dead because they cannot do these things.

The presence of a dead body is considered a source of ritual impurity. For this reason, the ancient Jewish priests could not be in the presence of a corpse. People who have been in the presence of a body wash their hands before entering a home. This is done to symbolically remove spiritual impurity, not physical uncleanness: it applies regardless of whether one has physically touched the body.

Preparation for Burial. In preparation for the burial the body is thoroughly cleaned and wrapped in a simple, plain linen shroud. The sages of Israel decreed that both the dress of the body and the coffin should be simple, so that a poor person would not receive less honor in death than a rich person. *The body is wrapped in a tallis/telet,* a replica lamb skin prayer shawl, with its *tzitzit* (fringes) rendered invalid.

The body is not embalmed and no organs or fluids may be removed. According to some sources, organ donation is permitted, because the subsequent burial of the *donee* will satisfy the requirement of burying the entire body.

Autopsies in general are discouraged as desecration of the body. However, autopsies are permitted when they may save a life or where local law requires it. When autopsies must be performed, they should be minimally intrusive.

The body must not be cremated. It must be buried in the earth. Coffins are not required, but if they are used, they must have holes drilled in them so the body comes in contact with the earth.

The body is never displayed at funerals; open casket ceremonies are forbidden by Jewish law. According to Jewish law, exposing a body is considered disrespectful, because it allows not only friends, but also enemies to view the dead, mocking their helpless state.

Jewish Mourning Practices.   Jewish mourning practices can be broken into several periods of decreasing intensity.

These mourning periods allow the full expression of grief, while discouraging excesses of grief and allowing the mourner to gradually return to a normal life. When a close relative first hears of the death of a relative, it is traditional to express the initial grief by tearing one's clothing. The tear is made over the heart if the deceased is a parent, or over the right side of the chest for other relatives. This tearing of the clothing is referred to as *keriyah* (lit. "tearing"). The mourner recites the blessing describing God as "the true Judge," an acceptance of God's taking of the life of a relative.

From the time of death to the burial, the mourner's sole responsibility is caring for the deceased and preparing for the burial. Judaism requires quick burial, so this period lasts 1-2 days **during which the family should be left alone** and allowed the full expression of grief. Condolence calls or visits should be made after this time.

When visiting a mourner, a guest should not try to express grief with standard, shallow platitudes. The guest should allow the mourner to initiate conversations. One should not divert the conversation from speaking about the deceased; to do so would limit the mourner's ability to fully express grief, which is the purpose of the mourning period. When leaving a house of mourning, it is traditional for the guest to say "May the Lord comfort you with all the mourners of Zion and Jerusalem."

Sitting *Shiva*. This begins the day of burial, continuing to the seventh day after burial. It is observed by parents, children, spouses and siblings of the deceased, preferably all together in the deceased's home. They sit on low stools or the floor, do not wear leather shoes, do not shave or cut their hair, do not wear cosmetics, do not work and do not do things for comfort or pleasure, such as bathe, have sex, put on fresh clothing, or study *Torah* (because it is a joy to study *Torah*). Mirrors in the house are covered during *Shiva*.

Tombstone. Jewish law requires that a tombstone be prepared so that the deceased will not be forgotten and the grave will not be desecrated. It is customary in some communities to keep the tombstone veiled, or to delay in putting it up until the end of the 12-month mourning period. There is generally a formal unveiling ceremony when the tombstone is revealed. It is customary to place small stones on a gravesite when visiting it. This may be where the practice of grave markers actually began.

Tish'ah Be-av

When the Temple of Solomon was destroyed, a mourning holiday, *Tish'ah Be-av*, was instituted and on that holiday lights are diminished. *Tish'ah Be-av* is the traditional day of mourning for the destruction of the Temples in Jerusalem. It is the culmination of the three weeks of mourning that start on the 17th of *Tammuz*. On *Tish'ah Be-av* in the year 586 B.C. the Babylonian king Nebuchadnezzar stormed the great Temple built by Solomon, turned its marbled columns and gilded rooms into a useless pile of rubble and exiled Jerusalem's inhabitants."

"This tragic day has therefore been set aside as a time of sadness for all Jews, who are required to fast the whole day and observe most of the mourning rites which apply in the case of a death in the family. At the evening service in the synagogue, all decorations are removed from the ark, the lights are dimmed, a few candles are lit, and the whole congregation sits on low benches or on the floor listening in hushed silence to the mournful notes of *Eikhah*, the Book of Lamentations written by the prophet Jeremiah, an eyewitness to the destruction of the first Temple." *(Encyclopedia Judaica Jr).*

BYU Professor of Ancient History Andrew C. Skinner has commented on the destruction of the Jewish temples of Babylon and Rome:

"Ever since, the Jerusalem temple has been the object of yearning for the Jewish people in all ages. Psalm 137, a hymn of the Israelite exiles from Jerusalem of the first temple period, continues to express the deepest sentiments of all Jews, both ancient and modern, and strikes a responsive chord among Mormons, who also comprehend and appreciate the magnitude of the disasters of 586 B.C. and 70 CE, precisely because their own historical circumstances of the nineteenth century have so sensitized them. The foundational literature of rabbinic Judaism...displays an obsession with the temple. Memories perpetuated by the rabbinic sages about God's holy house and the environment associated with it seem to have become so idealized and created such a powerful image that they took on a life of their own." *Andrew C. Skinner:* <u>The Inextricable Link Between Temple, Covenant, and Chosenness</u> *in Covenant and Chosenness in Judaism and Mormonism, p.77. Ed. Jospe, Madsen and Ward, 2001.*

The temple is part of the collective unconscious of the Jewish people. It figures prominently in Jewish wedding feasts, the celebration of *Chanukah*, *Yom Kippur* and the Passover seder. In ancient Israel the temple mount was inviolable. In Ezekiel 44:9, the prophet declared:

Thus saith the Lord God; No stranger, uncircumcised in heart, nor uncircumcised in flesh, shall enter into my sanctuary.

Skinner adds: "Only those who were qualified could participate in the sanctity of that holy place. So it is today with Mormon members who have to produce 'certification of their membership and worthiness within the covenant community before they can gain entry into a dedicated, hallowed temple of God. Possession of this certificate, which Mormons call a 'temple recommend,' is an important symbol of commitment to God and to fellow members of the covenant community—much like tangible witness of circumcision in Ezekiel's day." *Skinner, Andrew C.: The Inextricable Link Between Temple, in Covenant, and Chosenness, p. 79.*

Hebrew Calendar

Months. The Jewish/Hebrew calendar is lunar, with each month beginning on the new moon. The new months used to be determined by observation. When the new moon was observed, the *Sanhedrin* declared the beginning of a new month. Notices were sent to messengers to tell people when the month began.

Numbering of Jewish Years. The year number on the Jewish calendar represents the number of years since the Creation of this world, calculated by adding up the ages of people in the Bible back to the time of Creation. However, this does not necessarily mean that the universe has existed for only 5600 years as we understand years. Many **Orthodox** Jews will readily acknowledge that the first six "days" of creation are not necessarily 24-hour days (indeed, a 24-hour day would be meaningless until the creation of the sun on the fourth "day"). Jews do not generally use the words "A.D." and "B.C." to refer to the years on the Gregorian calendar. "A.D." means essentially "the year of our Lord." Jews do not believe Jesus is the Lord. Instead, they use the abbreviations C.E. (Common or Christian Era) and B.C.E. (Before the Common Era). The Gregorian year 2004 is equal to the Hebrew year 5764-5765. This is based upon the Jewish belief that the world began in 3761 B.C.

The Hebrew calendar has the following structure:

Month Name	Number	Length	Gregorian Equivalent
Nisan	1	30 days	March-April
Iyar	2	29 days	April-May
Sivan	3	30 days	May-June
Tammuz	4	29 days	June-July
Av	5	30 days	July-August
Elul	6	29 days	August-September
Tishri	7	30 days	September-October
Cheshvan	8	29 or 30 days	October-November
Kislev	9	30 or 29 days	November-December
Tevet	10	29 days	December-January
Shevat	11	30 days	January-February
Adar	12	29-30 days	February-March

Month Name	Number	Length	Gregorian Equivalent
Adar *II*	13	29 days	March-April

Jewish Recipes

Basic Blintzes (a filled, rolled and fried type of crepe) Makes about 12 large or 15 small blintzes. This is an Ashkenazic food, a specialty in Jewish homes throughout the world. There can be a great variety of fillings, from sweet to vegetarian, but the most common are the cheese blintzes, served as entrees or desserts and with sour cream and applesauce.

You can make the batter in a blender and it can keep a couple of days in the frig, or be frozen. Jews eat them hot or cold. They can be served with potato latkes (recipe follows) or about any other light dish.

> *3 large eggs*
> *About 1 2/3 cup milk,*
> *¾ cup all purpose flour, sifted*
> *½ tsp salt*
> *Oil for the pan*

To make by hand, push flour to sides of medium bowl, leaving a large well in center of flour. Add eggs, salt and ¼ cup milk to well; whisk them briefly until blended. Using the whisk, gradually stir flour into egg mixture until mixture is smooth. Gradually whisk in 1cup milk. Cover and refrigerate about 1 hour or up to 1 day. (Strain batter if lumpy). When you're ready to sauté the blintzes, melt butter in micro or small saucepan over low heat. Stir batter well. Gradually whisk melted butter into batter. It should have consistency of whipping cream. If too thick, gradually whisk in more milk, about 1 teaspoon at a time. Lastly, sauté butter to make blintzes.

To cook blintzes: Heat a 6 to 6 ½ inch crepe pan or skillet (for large blintzes use an 8-9 inch pan) over medium high heat. Sprinkle pan with a few drops of water. If water immediately sizzles, pan in hot enough. Brush pan lightly with oil. Remove pan from heat and hold it near bowl of batter. Quickly Add 2 tablespoons batter to pan; Add batter to edge of pan and tilt and swirl pan until base is covered with a thin layer of batter. Immediately pour any excess batter back into bowl.

Return pan to medium high heat. Loosen edges of blintz with metal spatula, discarding pieces clinging to sides of pan. Cook until bottom browns very lightly. Slide blintz onto a plate with uncooked side facing up. Top with sheet of wax paper or foil if desired. Reheat pan a few seconds.

Continue making blintzes, stirring batter occasionally with whisk. adjust heat and brush pan with more oil if necessary. If batter thickens on standing, very gradually whisk in a little more milk or water, about 1 teaspoon at a time. Pile blintzes on plate as they are done.

Potato Latkes (pancakes)
Makes about 8-10 servings
2 ½ lbs potatoes (about 8 large)
2 medium onions
2 large eggs
1 tsp salt
¼ c all purpose flour
Olive oil for frying (or PAM)

Preheat oven to 250º F. Line a tray with paper towels for draining latkes and have a baking sheet ready for keeping latkes warm.

Peel and grate potatoes and onions on large holes of a grater or similar tool. Alternate the onion and potato. Transfer grated mass to a colander. Squeeze mixture by handfuls until liquid is removed, as much as possible. Put potato-onion mixture in bowl. Add eggs, salt and flour. Mix well.

Heat oil in deep, large heavy skillet and drop about 2-3 tbsp of potato-onion mixture into pan. Flatten with back of spoon so each pancake is roughly 3" in diameter. Don't crowd in pan. Fry over medium heat 4-5 minutes on each side, or until crisp and golden brown. Turn carefully with two slotted spatulas so oil doesn't splatter. Transfer to paper towels. Stir batter before frying each new batch. Add more oil as necessary and heat it before Adding more latkes. Put the finished latkes on the tray and keep warm in your oven. Pat latkes with toweling before serving. Also very good cold. Serve with applesauce and/or sour cream.

Chicken Soup
2 ½ to 3 lbs chicken pieces, fat and skin removed
Salt and pepper (if desired)
1 large onion, sliced
6 medium carrots cut into 2-inch lengths
4 large cloves garlic
About 2 quarts water
2 ribs celery, cut into thin crosswise strips
½ cup long grain rice

Put chicken in large stew pan or pot. Sprinkle with salt, pepper. Add onion, carrots, celery, garlic and water. Bring to boil. Cover and cook over low heat, skimming foam occasionally, one hour. Skim off fat. Add rice about 15-20 minutes before serving. Remove chicken, cut meat from bones, and return meat to soup. Serve with challah or rolls and blintzes.

Recipes from *1,000 Jewish Recipes, by Faye Levy, IDG Books Worldwide, 2000.* Highly recommended with many wonderful recipes.

Jewish Jokes

One of the first things to realize about Jewish humor is that there are stereotypes. One of them is the Jewish mother who is usually portrayed as obsessive/compulsive over her husband and children, especially her sons. Guilt is a tactic she will use to remind her children of their filial duties. Because sons go out of the home and into the world, Jewish mothers feel neglected. They are experts at transmitting these feelings to their sons. Hence the following typical joke:

A Jewish man called his mother in Florida.

He said to his mother, "How are you doing?"

She said, "Not too good. I've been very weak."

The son then asked, "Why are you so weak?"

She said, "Because I haven't eaten in 38 days."

The son then asked, "Why you haven't eaten in 38 days?"

She said, "Because I didn't want my mouth to be filled with food when you called."

ψψψψψψψψψ

Why aren't there any Jewish mothers on parole boards?

They'd never let anyone finish a sentence.

ψψψψψψψψψ

What's Jewish Alzheimer's disease?

It's when you forget everything but the guilt.

ψψψψψψψψψ

Another Jewish stereotype is the smart Jews who outwits his captors, his government, his wife, Gentiles, the rich bankers, the whole world. These two jokes are typical of that mindset.

The phone rings at KGB headquarters.

"Hello? Hello, is this KGB?"

"Yes. What do you want?"

"I'm calling to report my neighbor Yankel Rabinovitz as an enemy of the State. He is hiding undeclared diamonds in his firewood."

"This will be noted."

Next day, the KGB comes over to Rabinovitz's house. They search the shed where the firewood is kept, break every piece of wood, find no diamonds, and swear at Yankel Rabinovitz and leave. The phone rings at Rabinovitz's house.

"Hello, Yankel! Did the KGB come?"

"Yes."

"Did they chop your firewood?"

"Yes, they did."

"Okay, now it's your turn to call. I need my vegetable patch plowed."

ษษษษษษษษษ

Three men, an Italian, a Frenchman, and a Jew, were condemned to be executed. Their captors told them that they had the right to a final meal of their choice before the execution.

They asked the Frenchman what he wanted. "Give me some good French wine and French bread," he requested. So they gave it to him, he ate it, and then they executed him.

Next it was the Italian's turn. "Give me a big plate of pasta," said the Italian. So they brought it to him, he ate it, and then they executed him.

Now it was the Jewish fellow's turn. "I want a big bowl of strawberries, " said the Jew.

"Strawberries! It's September. Strawberries aren't in season for months!" exclaimed his captors.

"So...I'll wait!"

ษษษษษษษษษ

My Jewish uncle Abe walks into a New York bank, and says he's going to Europe for two weeks and needs to borrow $5,000. For collateral, he offers his new Rolls Royce. The bank is satisfied and parks it in their secured underground garage.

Two weeks later to the day, Uncle Abe returns to the bank, repays the $5,000 and interest of $15.41. The loan officer says, "Mr. Sims, we were delighted to have your business but, in checking your credit, we learned you are a multimillionaire. Why ever did you need to borrow $5,000?"

My smart Uncle Abe said: "Where else in New York can I park my car for two weeks for $15.41?

שׁשׁשׁשׁשׁשׁשׁשׁ

This next joke is just plain fun. Jews usually think all Gentiles are in the same league, as Catholics and they love to poke fun at them and their rituals.

A Jewish man moves into a Catholic neighborhood. Every Friday the Catholics go crazy because, while they're morosely eating fish, the Jew is outside barbecuing steaks. So the Catholics work on the Jew to convert him. Finally, by threats and pleading, the Catholics succeed. They take the Jew to a priest who sprinkles holy water on the Jew and intones:

"Born a Jew.... Raised a Jew.... Now a Catholic."

The Catholics are ecstatic. No more delicious, but maddening smells every Friday evening. But the next Friday evening, the scent of barbecue wafts through the neighborhood. The Catholics all rush to the Jew's house to remind him of his new diet. They see him standing over the cooking steak. He is sprinkling water on the meat and saying:

"Born a cow.... Raised a cow.... Now a fish."

שׁשׁשׁשׁשׁשׁשׁשׁ

It seems that Jews love to eat at Chinese restaurants. This is not too unusual when you remember the Chinese are a different kind of goyim (non-Jew). They don't sprinkle water on babies or display crosses, their motif is Oriental and non-threatening, they are also successful businessmen, they are not anti-Semitic, and their egg rolls remind Jews of dried up blintzes.

I remember my visit to a Chinese restaurant recently with a Jewish friend. She asked if there are any Jews in China. "I don't know," I said. "Why don't we ask the waiter?"

When the waiter came by, she asked "Are there any Chinese Jews?"

"I don't know, let me ask," the waiter replied, and he went into the kitchen. He returned in a few minutes and said, "No. No Chinese Jews." "Are you sure?" she asked.

"I will check again, the waiter said and went back to the kitchen.

While he was still gone, I said "I can't believe there are no Jews in China. Our people are scattered everywhere."

The waiter came back, "Sorry, no Chinese Jews."

"How can that be", I asked.

"But I asked everyone," the waiter said. "We have orange Jews, prune Jews, tomato Jews and grape Jews, but no one ever hear of Chinese Jews!"

ושׁושׁושׁושׁושׁושׁושׁ

Significant Sources

Ancient Tablets to Modern Translations: General Introduction To The Bible
David Ewert, Zondervan Publishing 1983

Apostasy to Restoration, Course Study for the Melchizedek Priesthood
Quorums of The Church of Jesus Christ of Latter-day Saints, T. Edgar
Lyon, Deseret Book Company, 1960

Atlas of Jewish History
Martin Gilbert, Dorset Press 1976

Book of Mormon and Old Testament Student Manuals
Church of Jesus Christ of Latter-day Saints, 1979, 1980

Chiasmus in the Book of Mormon
John W. Welch, Ph.D., BYU Studies 1969

Code of Jewish Law
Orach Chaim 223:6 Rema ad loc.

The Complete Dead Sea Scrolls in English
Geza Vermes, Penguin Books 1995

Covenant and Chosenness in Judaism and Mormonism
Raphael Jospe, Truman G. Madsen, Seth Ward, Editors
Farleigh Dickinson University Press, 2001

Discovering Lehi, New Evidence of Lehi and Nephi in Arabia
Lynn M. Hilton and Hope A. Hilton, Cedar Fort, Incorporated, 1996.

Drama of the Lost Disciples
George F. Jowett, Covenant Publishing, 1961

The Gift of *Kaballah*: Discovering the Secrets of
Heaven, Renewing Your Life on Earth
Tamar Frankiel, Ph.D. , Jewish Light Publishing 2003

The Gospel in the Feasts Of Israel
Victor Buksbazen, Christian Literature Crusade, 1954

The Great Apostasy,
James E. Talmadge, Deseret Book Company, 1958

Hebraisms in the Book of Mormon: A Preliminary Survey
John A. Tvedtnes 1970

Israel! Do You Know?
LeGrand Richards, Deseret Book, 1954

Jesus The Christ
James E. Talmadge, Deseret Book Company, 1982

The Jewish Dietary Laws
Isidore Grunfeld, Soncino Press, London

The Joys of Yiddish
Leo Rosten, McGraw Hill, 1970

Judaism, Development and Life
Leo Trepp, Wadsworth Publishing, 1982

The Scriptures
CD, Intellectual Reserve, Inc. 2001

Literature of Belief: Sacred Scripture and Religious Experience
Ed. Neal E. Lambert, Religious Studies Center
Religious Studies Monograph Series, #5, Brigham Young University 1981

Mormons and Jews: Early Mormon Theologies of Israel
Steven Epperson, Signature Books, 1992

The Concise Guide to Judaism; History, Practice, Faith
Rabbi Roy A. Rosenberg, Meridian Books, 1994

The New Strong's Exhaustive Concordance of The Bible
James Strong LLD, STD, Thomas Nelson Publishers 1996

The Prophetic Book of Mormon
Hugh Nibley, FARMS, Deseret Book 1989

Responsa Nodah Biyehudah
Rabbi Yechezkel Landau, Yoreh Deah 10
Shechita: Religious, Historical and Scientific Perspectives,

Munk, Feldheim Publishers, New York, 1976

The Standard Works of the Church of Jesus Christ of Latter-day Saints
Study Aid for The Scriptures
Church Of Jesus Christ of Latter-day Saints
© 2001 Intellectual Reserve, Inc.

Internet Links and Insightful Readings

http://www.jewishconvert-lds.com   The author's home website.

http://www.peopleofthebook-judaica.com   The author's interfaith research website.

Links to Jewish websites

http://www.ldsjews.org

http://www.encyclopediajudaica.com

http://www.jewishencyclopedia.com

http://www.613.org a source of educational Orthodox Jewish audio and video files, all available for free viewing online using RealPlayer!

http://www.us-israel.org An activist organization to strengthen the U.S.-Israel relationship by emphasizing the values our nations share.

http://www.godaven.com A worldwide database of Orthodox prayer groups

http://www.jewishencyclopedia.com Contains contents of the 12-volume Jewish Encyclopedia.

http://www.jewishgen.org Home of Jewish Genealogy An excellent resource for researching your family history!

http://www.jewfaq.org Tracey R. Rich is the author of this excellent site. Credit is due him for some of the text I used.

http://www.maven.co.il A search engine of Jewish and Israel websites. Has perpetual lunar calendars, explanations.

http://www.us-israel.org Many useful information about Israel and Jewry.

http://www.messianicjewish.net Representative website involved with the ministries of International Messianic Jewish Alliance.

http://judaism.miningco.com A great resource for Jewish information with extensive links.

http://www.nazarene.net A website devoted to Nazarene Judaism

http://www.shamash.org A little bit of everything!

Magazines
John P. Pratt: The Restoration of Priesthood Keys On Easter, 1836, Part 2
Ensign, July 1985, p. 55.

"Israel My Glory," July-August 2003.

Books On Judaism For Inquirers
Tanakh: A New Translation of the Holy Scriptures
Jewish Publication Society

The Stone Tanach
Mesorah Publications

The Pentateuch and HafTorahs
Edited by Dr. J.H. Hertz, Soncino Press

To Be a Jew
Rabbi Hayim Halevy Donin, Basic Books

The Jewish Primer (Hardcover)
Rabbi Dr. Shmuel Himelstein, Facts on File

Basic Judaism
Milton Steinberg, Harcourt Brace Jovanovich

The First Jewish Catalog
Richard Siegel et al, Jewish Publication Society

The Joys of Yiddish
Leo Rosten, Pocket Books

Heritage: Civilization and the Jews
Abba Eban, Summit Books, VHS, DVD

Jewish Cookery
Leah W. Leonard, Crown Publishers

The Artscroll Siddur (Siddur Kol Yaakov)
Mesorah Publications

Everyman's *Talmud*
Cohen, Schocken Books

The Illustrated History of the Jewish People
Nicholas De Lange, Editor

Index

About the Author

Marlena Tanya Muchnick is a Jewish convert to the Church. She was baptized a Latter-day Saint April 6, 1988.

Marlena was raised in southern California in a Jewish family of Ukrainian ancestry. Feeling there was more to God's plan for her life, she began to search for answers. Her younger brother, a member, sent missionaries to teach her, but it was years later that her true conversion occurred. Sensing it was urgent she know if the Gospel and its restoration is truth, Marlena isolated herself, reading and praying for knowledge. She received her testimony and revelation instructing her to serve as a missionary for Christ.

Marlena gives firesides throughout America about her conversion experience, her testimony and her fervent love for the Savior. These talks convey helpful information about Judaism. She also enjoys presenting Seminary and Institute talks as well as informal informational gatherings and Passover *Seder* demonstrations. Please visit her website to set up a presentation in your ward, stake, or mission.

Ms Muchnick's published softcover books, tapes, CD's and songs are available through LDS and other bookstores online, Ebay, and from the author through her websites below. These currently include:

- Notes of A Jewish Convert to the LDS Church: Conversion of A Soul
- Life Changing Testimonies of the Lord Jesus Christ
- Adventures With the Angels of Love
- People of The Book (*Am ha-Sefer Torah*). Also available in tape and CD set
- A Mormon's Guide to Judaism
- Dynamics of Freedom: 7 ½ hour sessions on Constitution. VHS
- Fireside addresses with original songs: DVD and tape for libraries and showings to congregations
- Original songs with sheet music
- Demo (on DVD) for preview by those interested in scheduling visits. Includes short sections: fireside talks, songs, Passover seder demonstration and nature of Judaism

www.jewishconvert-lds.com

www.peopleofthebook-judaica.com